Beyond the Quiet Time

Beyond the
Quiet Time

Practical Evangelical Spirituality

ALISTER McGRATH

Baker Books

A Division of Baker Book House Co
Grand Rapids, Michigan 49516

Published by Baker Books
a division of Baker Book House Company
P.O. Box 6287, Grand Rapids, MI 49516-6287

First printing, April 1996

Published by arrangement with SPCK, London

Printed in the United States of America

Library of Congress Cataloging-in-Publication Data

McGrath, Alister E., 1953–
    Beyond the quiet time : practical evangelical spirituality / Alister McGrath.
       p.   cm.
    Includes bibliographical references.
    ISBN 0-8010-5708-6
    1. Spiritual life—Christianity—Study and teaching. 2. Spiritual-ity—Study and teaching. 3. Devotional exercises. I. Title.
BV4511.M44 1996
248.4'07—dc20   96-7030

*For the faculty and students of
Regent College, Vancouver*

CONTENTS

PREFACE

Vancouver is Canada's most secular city, yet it is also home to one of the most vibrant and dynamic Christian communities in the world. Since it first opened for full-time study in 1970, Regent College has established itself as one of the largest and most influential graduate schools of theology. Under the direction of its first principal, former Oxford academic James M. Houston, the college has gained an international reputation as a place where the Christian laity may gain a first-rate theological education.

However, it is now also gaining a reputation for something else. In the last five years, Regent College has begun to emerge as a laboratory in which new evangelical approaches to Christian spirituality are devised and tested. This process has been stimulated in part by its two professors of spiritual theology, James Houston and Eugene Peterson, and given rigour by leading faculty members such as James I. Packer. Year after year, hundreds of ordinary Christians, thirsting for a deepened understanding and appreciation of their faith, flock to its courses and summer schools. Like tired and thirsty travellers in a desert, they sense that Regent College offers a spiritual oasis; they go home refreshed and renewed. Thus the college is now widely recognized as a crucible in which forms of Christian spirituality, steeped in the evangelical tradition yet relating to the needs and pressures of a highly fragmented Western culture, are being developed. It is a wonderfully exciting environment in which to work, and I have found that my own thinking on spirituality, both in theory and practice, has been enormously stimulated and informed through my association with the college.

What I propose to offer in this little book is an attempt to develop an approach to spirituality, suitable for individuals or groups, that is firmly rooted in the great evangelical tradition, yet adapted to our modern needs. The format, structure, and contents of the book have been based on extensive discussions with colleagues in London, Los Angeles, Melbourne, Oxford, Sydney, Toronto, and Vancouver, linked with experience of practical application and evaluation of the approaches developed in this book. It makes full use of the empathetic and imaginative techniques developed by writers such as Robert M. Banks (Fuller Theological Seminary), and James Houston and Eugene Peterson (Regent College, Vancouver), while maintaining the strongly doctrinal core of evangelicalism.

This book adopts an evangelical approach to spirituality, and it is therefore appropriate to explain what 'evangelical' means. Evangelicalism is a form of Christianity which is committed to the great themes of traditional Christian faith, and places special emphasis on a series of central themes and concerns, including the following:

- a focus, both devotional and theological, on the person of Jesus Christ, especially his death on the cross;
- the identification of Scripture as the ultimate authority in matters of spirituality, doctrine and ethics;
- an emphasis upon conversion or a 'new birth' as a life-changing religious experience;
- a concern for sharing the faith, especially through evangelism.

It will therefore be clear that the way in which Scripture is used in spirituality will be of central importance to evangelicals. In the past, evangelicals have tended to place emphasis on the 'Quiet Time' – that is, a daily period set aside for reading and meditating on Scripture. This book aims to maintain the distinctive evangelical emphasis on Scripture, yet adopt approaches which avoid the weaknesses of the traditional 'Quiet Time'.

The title of this book reflects a widespread feeling, particularly among younger Christians, that the traditional 'Quiet Time' has become tired and problematic. Obviously the basic principle of being spiritually nourished and encouraged by Scripture remains of central importance; it is simply that traditional methods of relating to Scripture have become unhelpful for some individuals. This book aims to develop an approach that affirms the centrality and vitality of Scripture in the Christian life, while exploring ways of relating to it that avoid the staleness of some older methods. Although those who find traditional approaches helpful may find this book useful, it is really aimed at those who feel the need for something fresh.

USING THIS BOOK IN GROUPS

This book has been designed to be an effective and stimulating resource for groups:

- The Introduction sets the scene for the book, by exploring some issues about evangelical spirituality; you will get more out of the study sessions if you read the introductory section first. The Introduction is not, however, meant for group study. So if you are leading group study based on this book, suggest that those in the group read the Introduction before your study session begins.
- Allow 1–1½ hours for each of the five study sessions. The precise length will depend on the extent to which people want to talk.
- If resources are available, you will find it helpful to have a short time of worship before and after each study session. The texts of any songs can easily be linked to the themes to be discussed.
- No other books or texts will be needed. Biblical texts of relevance are printed out in full, in the New International Version.
- It will be helpful if you have pen and paper to hand.
- Appoint someone as leader. The leader's chief function will be to read sections aloud, or to ask others to do so, and to direct discussion using the prompts provided.
- | **Pause** | marked in the text is an invitation to stop and reflect on the issue concerned. At this point, the leader asks people to discuss the subject indicated by the text. When the leader feels that the discussion has gone far enough, the study can be resumed. The book is intended to help people share experiences and insights, and discussion is a vital means by which this can take place.
- The questions you are asked to discuss are often answered in the material that follows. This is because these questions are meant to help you deepen your own understanding and appreciation of the gospel by getting you to talk or think.

- At several points, the text asks you to imagine a scene, and provides short sentences to help you build up a mental picture. The leader should read these out slowly and clearly, with a pause of a minute or so between them, to allow people to absorb the ideas, and stimulate their thought.
- The exercise or exercises at the end of each study session are an important element of each section; they are there to be used. However, the leader may find that pressure of time means that only some, if any, can be used in the study session. If so, ask members of the group to work on the others in their own time. If the book is being used as a retreat resource, the exercises can be built into the structure of the retreat itself.
- The 'Study Panels' are there to provide information that can either be built into the study, or that can be read by members in their own time.

USING THIS BOOK ON YOUR OWN

This book provides an ideal resource for a traditional 'Quiet Time', while avoiding the problems that many people have concerning it. Such problems include an awareness of the need for more help and guidance than is normally given, and the stress on analysing the text, rather than appreciating its spiritual importance. It is hoped that the approach adopted here will be both stimulating and helpful.

- The Introduction sets the scene for the book, by exploring some issues about evangelical spirituality; you will get more out of the study sessions if you read the introductory section first. It is because the Introduction is so different in tone and approach from the remainder of the book that you are strongly urged to read it first. If you want to, you can treat the Introduction itself as material for a 'Quiet Time'.
- No other texts will be needed. Biblical texts of relevance are printed out in full, in the New International Version.
- It will be helpful if you have pen and paper to hand.
- $\boxed{\textit{Pause}}$ marked in the text is an invitation to stop ar ⌐ reflect on the issue being discussed. This pause co⌐'.. take the form of making yourself a cup of coffee, ⌐ going for a walk, while you reflect on the points being raised. When you feel ready to do so, you can come back to the text.
- The questions on which you are asked to reflect are often answered in the material that follows. This is because these questions are meant to help you deepen your own understanding and appreciation of the gospel by getting you to think about the issues, or talk about them with others.
- At several points, the text asks you to imagine a scene, and provides short sentences to help you build up a mental picture. Read these to yourself slowly and clearly, pausing between them, to allow yourself to absorb the ideas, and stimulate your thought.

- The exercise or exercises at the end of each study session are an important element of each section; they are there to be used. Treat them as an important component of your 'Quiet Time'.
- The 'Study Panels' should be read as part of your 'Quiet Time'. They relate to the text, and provide background material that will bring added depth to your study.

INTRODUCTION

This book is not about the history of spirituality; nor is it about the theory of spirituality. Instead, this book is about *doing* spirituality. Yet what does that mean? Well, for a start it means:

- Discovering the full richness of our faith.
- Developing ways of keeping our faith alive and growing.

Often we take our faith for granted; we have got used to it. It is like an old chair, which feels familiar and comfortable most of the time, yet gets tired and weary and needs restoring from time to time. It is like a friendship or a marriage – it needs bringing to life again every now and then. If our faith is going to work, it needs nourishment and enrichment.

What is spirituality?

'Spirituality' is the term that is now being used throughout Western society to refer to ways of rediscovering the spiritual aspects of life. However, not all spirituality is Christian! Many forms of spirituality that are found in North America and else-where owe many of their ideas to Buddhist or Native American spirituality.[1] For example, the Buddhist idea of meditating through emptying the mind of all its thoughts stands in contrast to the Christian idea of allowing the mind to focus on Jesus Christ. This book deals with Christian spirituality, from an evangelical perspective. A Christian spirituality focuses on the deepening of the life of faith in relation to Jesus Christ, recognizing in him the fullness of life that God wishes his people to possess.

In its specifically Christian sense, the word 'spirituality' focuses on the 'spiritual person' (*pneumatikos anthrōpos*) (1 Corinthians 2.14–15) – that is, the person who has faith in the risen Christ, and is in the process of being renewed through the work of the Holy Spirit. In its Christian sense, 'spirituality' is about the process of renewal and rebirth that comes about through the action of the Holy Spirit, which makes us more like Christ. It is about spiritual growth and development, and includes the development of just about every aspect of our life of Christian faith. The term also refers to the development of ways of reading and engaging with Scripture that are intended to nourish and sustain the life of faith, and especially to enable it to grow, even in adverse conditions.

For the Christian, spirituality has a twofold focus. First, it focuses on Jesus Christ. Many Christians find it helpful to focus on the ministry of Jesus, such as the way in which he shows God's love for people through his dealings with them. Others focus on Jesus' sufferings and death on the cross. This approach, which is characteristic of evangelicalism, lays emphasis on the costliness and reality of our redemption. Others focus on the resurrection of Christ, and the great hope that this brings to life. This emphasis on the importance of Jesus distinguishes Christian spirituality from other types.

Second, Christian spirituality puts an emphasis on the reading of Scripture. For the Christian, reading Scripture is like reading a book about a close and dear personal friend. Every page is important, because it tells you more and more about someone who matters to you – and *you* matter to them as well! So it is natural that you want to learn more about this person, so that you can draw closer to them. Scripture assists us in understanding more about God and his purposes for us. It helps us to appreciate the wonder and privilege of knowing God. And it tells us more about the person of Jesus Christ, who stands at the centre of our faith. For reasons such as this, Bible Study groups have always been at the heart of evangelical Christianity. In recent years, the Bible Study group has become even more important, as people have realized how small groups are a stimulus to church growth.

Other writings can be useful in helping us to deepen our grasp of Scripture, and many hymns offer memorable or inspiring paraphrases of complex biblical passages. Older hymns in particular can provide deeply moving meditations on the suffering and death of Jesus Christ, a theme that is always of central importance to evangelical spirituality. Biblical commentaries also aid our understanding of scriptural passages; and great Christian writers, both past and present, can help us reflect on the meaning and application of Scripture.

Yet we need to appreciate that these hymns, commentaries, and writers are not substitutes for Scripture. Instead, they are like lenses that help us to bring biblical ideas into perspective. They are like signposts, which point us to a renewed engagement with, and appreciation of, Scripture. Evangelicalism has no place for those 'spiritual' writers who point us away from Scripture or Jesus Christ. Their reliability and trustworthiness is to be judged by the extent to which such writers are Christ-centred and scripturally focused.

Why does 'spirituality' matter?

The eighteenth century saw great revivals take place within Christianity in England and in North America, and one of the most important of these was the 'Great Awakening' in eighteenth-century Massachusetts. Although this revival initially centred on Jonathan Edwards, a local pastor, it soon spread far beyond this. People came to faith in large numbers, and the level of crime plummeted. Yet coming to faith is one thing; *growing* in faith is another. At this time, a young woman convert wrote a letter to Jonathan Edwards. She had come to faith, she explained; but now she needed guidance, as she put it, as to 'the best manner of *maintaining* a religious life'.

Conversion is about the start of the Christian life; but we need to go on from there, and to develop. Faith is like a seed: it has the capacity to grow. If it is planted, it will flourish. However, it needs to be nourished and tended, and spirituality is about the nourishing and tending of personal faith. It is about keeping people going and growing in their faith. That means helping people to develop approaches and disciplines that will make sure that their faith is not stunted like a neglected plant, but is set free to achieve the full potential that God wants us to have.

Think of the parable of the sower (Mark 4.3–20). This parable tells of the seed (which we learn represents the word of God) being planted in the earth. In some cases, the seed grows rapidly, then withers on account of the shallowness of its roots. In other cases, it springs up, only to be choked by the weeds. Yet it is the same seed that has been planted in each case. Spirituality is doing everything possible on our part to ensure that the seed of the gospel takes root in our lives. Of course, God has a central and vital role to play in this process of germination and growth; but we have our part to play as well. 'Spirituality' refers to the methods we can develop to make sure that we are providing the best possible soil for the gospel to become established and to grow.

Learning from the past

One resource that is of vital importance in Christian spirituality is the past. Men and women have lived the Christian life before us, and have passed down to us their insights and ideas about living the Christian life in all its fullness. Reading the thoughts of the great Christians of the past can bring new depth to our faith and understanding. In some ways, it is like being at a really good Bible Study! Imagine that you are at a Bible Study, and are talking about a passage or some issue that arises from it, but that you are not getting very far. Then suddenly, someone in the group speaks up; and as she speaks, you realize that what she is saying is really helpful. People start to nod their heads. What is happening? What difference is this person making?

First, she may *explain* something well, allowing you to really understand it for the first time; or she may use an illustration or analogy that brings a biblical passage or idea to life; or perhaps she describes an experience in her life when a particular biblical idea or passage really helped her. As you listen, you realize that without her contribution, you would have missed out on something. The approach adopted in this book will thus allow you to study the Bible in good company!

Yet there is a more important point than this. We need to be reminded that between us and the first Christians there is a great stream of faithful women and men, who ran the Christian race before us. Listening to the great Christians of the past is about honouring those who walked the Christian path before us. It is about realizing that there is a great 'cloud of witnesses' who have wrestled with the issues of Christian living and thinking, and that we can learn from them. Here's how John of Salisbury, a twelfth-century English writer, put this point: 'We are like dwarves sitting on the shoulders of giants. We see more things than them, and things that are farther away – not because we can see better than them, or because we are taller than they are, but because they raise us up, and add their stature to ours'. So think of today's Christians as being able to climb up on the shoulders of men and women from the past, and learning from their wisdom – as well as their mistakes!

Spirituality and everyday life

People often complain about a lack of connection between their faith and everyday life. This is especially the case in Western society, where the pressures of our working lives often seem to lead to faith being relegated to some kind of watertight compartment, and isolated from the rest of life. One of the greatest challenges to Christian spirituality is to develop approaches that help people make the links between faith and everyday life.

However, there is a paradox here. Jesus Christ himself used everyday events and images to present the good news of the Kingdom of God. Things that everyone was familiar with from everyday life – like the planting of seeds, the lighting of lamps, or finding something that had been lost – become channels for the good news. Yet we seem to have managed an inverse miracle, by breaking that connection! Somehow, our faith seems to get cut off from everyday life. Yet in the preaching of Jesus Christ, there is a natural connection between the two. We have a lot to rediscover here!

The same thing goes for the words that St Paul uses to talk about the great benefits that Jesus Christ won for us by his death and resurrection. In his letters, Paul often talks about 'redemption', 'salvation', 'adoption', and 'reconciliation'. Yet we often treat these words like jargon – we behave as if they are just some kind of technical words that Christians use! When St Paul used these words in his letters, though, he expected them to bring his readers' faith to life. Each of them is drawn from the everyday life of the period, and paints a brilliant picture of what it means to be a Christian. Yet, partly through laziness and partly through overfamiliarity, we have lost sight of the vividness and power of these images. We need to rediscover them – it is like polishing old coins until they shine again!

When I was at school, we used to enjoy playing around with dangerous chemicals in the school laboratory. The more dangerous they were, the greater the excitement in using them! One of the more 'amusing' tricks (or so it seemed at the time!) was to get a really old copper coin, and drop it in a beaker of dilute nitric acid. The acid would turn blue, and give off very unpleasant fumes. As these fumes dispersed, the coin would appear as if it were new. The acid had dissolved the dirt and grime that had obscured the features of the coin. The coins that we used for this experiment were old British pennies, which had the image of Queen Victoria stamped upon them. This image was initially totally invisible, on account of the layers of dirt that had built up over the decades. Although the image was there, it could not be seen. By getting rid of this accumulated debris, the acid restored the image so that it was clearly and brilliantly visible. The same is true for the images that the Bible uses to help us understand and to get excited about our faith; they have got covered with dirt. Yet we need to make them shine again! We need to bring them back to life!

'Being active' and 'being receptive'

Evangelicalism is strongly activist, and this has enormous advantages. It means that evangelicals gladly throw themselves into the tasks of the Christian life. They are fully involved in the great missionary tasks of the Church, and they are committed to the pastoral, social, and evangelistic ministry of the gospel. The massive expansion of evangelicalism worldwide since the Second World War is partly a result of the willingness of evangelicals to be actively involved in Christian ministry, despite heavy work loads and responsibilities in the everyday world. Evangelicals passionately want to do something for God.

Yet God also wants to do something for evangelicals! There is a real danger that evangelicals will be so busy doing things for God that they will crowd him out by their very activity! Our desire to do things for God can easily get in the way of God's desire to do something for us. To be active in the world we must be receptive towards God – and that means making space to listen to God, to read the Bible, and to come before him, expecting to receive guidance, encouragement, and nourishment. The price paid for evangelical activism is all too often nothing other than evangelical burn-out. The 'I-feel-guilty-when-I'm-not-busy' syndrome is a sure sign of someone who is heading down the road that leads to exhaustion and uselessness.

There is no secret about *how* this is to be avoided, just as there is no doubt that it *must* be avoided. We need to create space for God in our lives, and that means discipline – an ability and willingness to dedicate part of each day to God, and not to allow anything else to get in its way. Spending quality time with God is the precondition for effective and sustainable Christian service in the world. We are indeed called to be the 'salt of the earth' (Matthew 5.13); but that salt can lose its saltiness, and what use is it then? We are called to be the 'light of the world' (Matthew 5.14) – but what use will we be if the cells powering that light become run down, so that the light fades and eventually goes out altogether? We need to renew our faith, yet that is something which, strictly speaking, only God can do. And that means giving God the openings to refresh and renew us with his grace and love. It means allowing him those windows of opportunity, through which he can break into our consciousness and make his presence felt in our lives.

The example of the church at Laodicea must be noted here (Revelation 3.14–22). This church was complacent and luke-warm; it needed renewing. Yet the risen Christ was knocking at the door of that church, asking to be admitted in order that he might renew it (Revelation 3.20). Some Christians tend to be too busy to hear that knocking. With a grim relentlessness, they keep on being passionately busy for Christ, unaware that the same Christ who they are trying to serve is just as passionately trying to refresh and renew them.

One possibility here is a retreat, yet many evangelical Christians react with alarm to this suggestion. We are meant to serve God in the world! To suggest that we 'retreat' from the world, they say, is therefore ridiculous. Certainly, there is much wisdom in that reaction; evangelicalism has been deeply influenced by the spirituality of the Reformation. During the sixteenth century, the centre of Christian living moved decisively from the monastery to the market place. Reformers such as John Calvin developed strongly world-affirming spiritualities that encouraged and enabled Christians to serve God in the everyday world.

Yet serving God in the world is tiring and often demoralizing. Christians need to be refreshed, to regain a sense of vision for their lives. In order to be of use to God in the world, it is necessary from time to time to withdraw from that world, and seek refreshment. The great ocean liner that safely transports passengers across the world's oceans regularly needs to return to port for refitting; the missionary on active service overseas needs to return home on furlough for rest. And Jesus Christ himself withdrew into the wilderness in order to pray (Luke 5.16).

A retreat is not a permanent withdrawal from the world. It is simply an oasis in a desert, a period of rejuvenation that allows us to return to the world with new strength and vision. In fact, it need only be a day. John Stott commends this practice, which transformed his own ministry at All Souls, Langham Place, in central London:

> I have discovered the immense profit of a quiet day at least once a month. I learned this from the Revd. L.F.E. Wilkinson during an address he gave at the Islington Clerical Conference in about 1951. It is the only thing I remember from the whole conference. But it came to me as a message from God. I had been precipitated into being Rector of All Souls at the age of twenty-nine, when I was much too young and inexperienced for such a responsibility. I began living from hand to mouth. Everything piled up and got on top of me. I felt crushed by the heavy administrative load. I started having the typical clerical nightmare: I was halfway up the pulpit steps when I realized that I had forgotten to prepare a sermon. Then came L.F.E. Wilkinson's address. 'Take a quiet day once a month,' he said, or words to that effect. 'Go away into the country, if you can, where you can be sure of being undisturbed. Stand back, look ahead, and consider where you are going. Allow yourself to be drawn up into the mind and perspective of God. Try to see things as he sees them. Relax!' I did. I went home, and immediately marked one day a month in my engagement book with the letter 'Q' for Quiet. And as I began to enjoy these days, the intolerable burden lifted and has never returned. . . . I could not exaggerate the blessing which these quiet days have brought to my life and ministry.[2]

Many Christians feel guilty about even the *idea* of a quiet day – 'We must *do* something!' has become a central part of their outlook. Yet this mentality is deeply destructive, and will simply lead to ineffective Christian living and ministry, and personal burn-out. Two reasons may be given for encouraging Quiet Days. First, God wants us to spend time with him; he wants to have our exclusive attention. He wants to matter to us as much as we matter to him. He wants us to set aside time for him alone, and nothing and nobody else. And second, we can only be effective Christian servants if we are close to the Lord, depending on him and drawing on his resources. Let us explore both these points.

Why did Jesus go into the wilderness to pray? The answer is that there were no distractions there – it was a place where only God would be found. By deliberately preventing ourselves from being distracted, we make it easier to break our addictive dependence on work and activity. Personally, I find long airline flights to be deeply refreshing; I look forward to the long flights between London and Australasia in a way that amazes my colleagues, who find them very boring and tiring. Yet those long flights are times when I can be on my own with God, with nothing to distract me. I can think about my life and ministry, and reflect on biblical passages and themes, in the sure knowledge that nobody can bother me. For me, they are nothing less than God-given times of renewal. Such times can be part of the life of any Christian. It is simply a matter of identifying them, and having the personal discipline to make the most of them.

Alongside this, there is also the crucial matter of acknowledging that we depend on God for everything in the life of faith. Prayer itself is a tacit acknowledgement that we need to rely on God, yet in our practical Christian living, we often behave as if God depends on us. The quality of our Christian life and witness is directly dependent on the quality of our relationship with God. To use the powerful image of the vine (John 15.1–8), we cannot bear fruit unless we remain attached to the vine. It is fatally easy to confuse 'being busy' with 'being right with God'. Allowing God to draw near to us is not an optional extra in the Christian life; it is the precondition of effective and fulfilled Christian living.

If you are dissatisfied with the quality of your Christian life, perhaps the first thing you need to sort out is the pressures of your everyday life. Start cutting back on the non-essentials, and stop pretending that you need to do everything. As has often been pointed out, the essence of sin is self-deceit. We easily deceive ourselves about things, as we prefer the make-believe world to the real one; and so we like to think that our presence and input is essential – that everyone else is dependent on our wisdom and guidance. However, this simply is not true. Start cutting back, pruning the branch of your vine so that it can bear more fruit. In 1979, the great evangelist Billy Graham told a startled audience in London that, if he had his ministry all over again, he would take on far fewer engagements. He said that his level of activity was high, but the quality was low. He needed more time to deepen the quality of his Christian ministry. We are being asked to do our best for God – and best is about quality, not quantity.

Yet spending time with God is not about abandoning Christian responsibilities! Some Christians seem to go on personal 'guilt trips' every time they are not being active in the world; yet they are *meant* to spend time with God. In fact, more than that: they are meant to *enjoy* him. As the *Westminster Shorter Catechism* puts it, our chief end is to 'glorify God and enjoy him for ever'. That is why we are here! Our responsibility is to glorify God; and our privilege is to enjoy him. Many Christians fail to realize the sheer delight of being able to spend quality time with God. As a result, they miss out on the profound biblical emphasis on the loveliness of God, and the privilege of being able to draw near to him. The sense of wonder and delight is expressed in passages such as the following: 'One thing I ask of the LORD, this is what I seek: that I may dwell in the house of the LORD all the days of my life, to gaze upon the beauty of the LORD and to seek him in his temple' (Psalm 27.4).

For St Paul, one of the greatest privileges of the Christian faith is our access to God (Romans 5.1–2), yet some Christians need to realize that this is more than a notional privilege. It is something that we are meant to make use of; we have the right to draw near to God on account of Christ's death and resurrection. Yet so often we are too busy to make use of this right. Is it surprising that we burn out so easily, when we neglect such a great and refreshing resource?

Ways of reading Scripture

The Bible can be read in different ways. It can be read as if it is primarily a textbook, or a source of information. This approach focuses on the need to deepen our understanding and knowledge of the Bible, and is of major importance to the Christian life. Alone, though, this approach is not enough. Reading the Bible in this way is like perusing a guidebook to another country: it provides you with interesting and important information – such as how to get there, how to cope with the language, and identifying things that are worth seeing. Yet reading the guidebook is no substitute for visiting that country. Only experiencing the country at first hand brings the guidebook to life. The guidebook is there to make your experience of that country as wonderful as possible, by explaining all that you need to know. Information and explanation, though, are definitely no substitute for experience.

The Christian life is about knowing God, and knowing God has both objective and subjective aspects. The objective aspects are knowing the nature and purposes of God. These things are true, and can be relied upon. The Christian faith is grounded in the total reliability and trustworthiness of God. Yet these truths of God are objective; they do not depend upon our feelings for their truth. Experience can easily be deceptive and misleading, which is why the objectivity of truth remains of essential importance to the Christian faith.

Yet there is also a subjective side to faith. The Christian faith is not simply about *knowing* the truth; it is about being *transformed* by the truth. As the Danish writer Søren Kierkegaard once wrote, there is a need for 'an appropriation process of the most passionate inwardness'.[3] To know God is to know about God, and to know and be known by God. We need to 'interiorize' the truths of Scripture. Where Scripture states truths, we must respond to them. Where Scripture describes the impact of Jesus Christ upon people, we must allow him to have that impact upon us as well.

It has often been said that Christianity consists of a personal relationship between Christ and the believer. Christian faith is not just about belief in the idea of God, but is also trust in the person of God. There is a story about the British philosopher Bertrand Russell. One day he was walking down one of Oxford's many lanes, thinking great philosophical thoughts, when he suddenly stopped, and said to himself: 'The ontological argument is right after all!' (In other words, he came to the conclusion that a certain philosophical proof for the existence of God was valid.) On another day, somewhat earlier in human history, Saul of Tarsus (who later became known as St Paul) was walking down a different road, when he encountered the risen Christ. Russell had an idea, but Saul met a *person*. There is all the difference in the world between these two experiences! Some years ago, the evangelist L. Stanley Jones became involved in a discussion with Mahatma Gandhi about the nature and relevance of Christianity. Gandhi, who played a major role in bringing about the formation of modern India, could see Jesus Christ as nothing other than a moral teacher. Gandhi was impressed by the moral teaching of Christ, and wrote to Jones to tell him so. Exasperated, Jones penned the following lines in reply: 'You have found the principles, yet missed the person'.

We can read the Bible as a guidebook to Jesus Christ, appreciating the way in which the many strands of the Old Testament find their fulfilment in him. Yet there is another way of reading the Bible, which supplements this. It is to read Scripture in order to deepen our relationship with Jesus Christ; and that means learning more about him (the objective side of things), and deepening our commitment and love for him (the subjective side of things). These two aspects are like the two sides of the same coin. They both need to be there. The head and the heart are both caught up in Christian faith.

This book aims to deepen both aspects of our faith, by appealing to both head and heart. It is fatally easy to read Scripture with the expectation that we will learn more about things such as the date of the fall of Jerusalem to the

Babylonians, or mourning customs in ancient Israel, or the precise geography of the Holy Land, or the routes of St Paul's second missionary journey. That information is certainly there, but it is the backdrop to something far more important, which is so easily missed: *that we need to read Scripture with the expectation that we will encounter, and be refreshed by, God.* We need to pause and savour each verse, drinking in its significance as if it were a precious vintage. We need to think ourselves into the situations being described, in order that we may grasp as much as possible of the experience of God that is being described. We must do everything we can to allow Scripture to address us and challenge us. It holds the key to our renewal; we must use it wisely.

Scripture was of central importance to the Reformation of the sixteenth century; and the reasons for this development are as complicated as they are fascinating.[4] One such reason is of importance to our discussion here. Many Christians in the late Middle Ages felt that the Church had lost sight of its reason for existence; that it had become an empty shell. Yet when such Christians read the New Testament, they noticed how it was saturated with the presence and power of the risen Christ. The contrast with their own experience could not have been more marked, for the risen Christ did not seem to feature very prominently in the life of the Church of the late Middle Ages.

And so dissatisfaction gradually gave way to vision. Why shouldn't the risen Christ be restored to his Church? Why shouldn't modern Christians be able to experience the same presence and power of the risen Christ as the first Christians? Why shouldn't the New Testament become a model for Christian life and experience in the present? And so the New Testament began to be read with a sense of expectation – expectation that the risen Christ would again be experienced by his Church, and fill that Church with his power and presence. The medieval Church was like the valley of dry bones. It had structure, but no vitality. Yet the New Testament offered the vision of a Church empowered and renewed by the presence of the risen Christ! Reading Scripture thus shaped the vision and heightened expectations, leading to the renewal and reform of the Church.

We need such a vision today. Reading Scripture can generate and nourish such a vision, and motivate us to work for renewal and growth, both personal and corporate.

The impact of the Enlightenment

About 1750, a major shift began to take place in Western Europe and North America as a new period in cultural history opened up. The period in question, known as the 'Enlightenment', would have a major impact on Christianity in those regions. This movement asserted that human reason was the only thing that really mattered; reason, it was argued, was capable of telling us everything we needed to know about God. The rise of the movement that is now generally known as 'postmodernism' throughout the Western world is a direct result of both the collapse of this confidence in reason and a more general disillusionment with the so-called 'modern' world. Postmodernism is the movement that proclaims that the Enlightenment rested on fraudulent intellectual foundations (such as the belief in the omnicompetence of human reason), and that it ushered in some of the most horrific events in human history – such as the Stalinist purges and the Nazi extermination camps. The new cultural mood that has developed since the 1980s has been a rebellion against the Enlightenment. Who wanted anything to do with an intellectually dubious movement that had given rise to such horrors?

There has thus been a widespread and gradual collapse of confidence in the Enlightenment trust in the power of reason. Yet many Christians have, probably without realizing it, been deeply influenced by the Enlightenment emphasis on reason. For example, some Christians continue to use approaches to evangelism that focus on an appeal to reason; yet those approaches were generally developed back in the early nineteenth century, as a response to the Enlightenment emphasis on reason. They were not typical of the spreading of the gospel before this time. However, now that the Enlightenment is over, we are free to recover older and more authentically evangelical approaches, rather than remaining trapped in a rationalist worldview.

The same is true of spirituality. Many Christians limit their spirituality to understanding the biblical text – that is, to reading it, making sense of its words and ideas, and understanding its historical background and its meaning for today. Thus the emphasis continues to be on reason. Yet we need to reach behind the Enlightenment, and recover older and more authentic evangelical approaches to spirituality, such as those found in the great Puritan writers such as Jonathan Edwards, or those of Pietist writers such as John and Charles Wesley. The Enlightenment placed an embargo on any kind of *emotional* involvement with Scripture, or any use of the human faculty of imagination – two approaches that earlier evangelicalism had treasured. Scripture was to be read as if it were a religious textbook, not a narrative of the love of God.

It is a well-known fact of history that Protestantism, in all its forms, was influenced by the rationalism of the Enlightenment to a far greater extent than, for example, Roman Catholicism or Eastern Orthodoxy. This has had a devastating impact on evangelical spirituality, and placed it at a serious disadvantage in relation to both Roman Catholic or Eastern Orthodox spiritualities. The Enlightenment forced evangelicalism into adopting approaches to spirituality that have resulted in rather cool, detached, and rational approaches to Scripture, such as those that have been associated with the traditional 'Quiet Time'.

Yet the Enlightenment is over, and we need to purge rationalism from within evangelicalism. And that means recovering the relational, emotional, and imaginative aspects of biblical spirituality that the Enlightenment declared to be improper. As Martin Luther constantly insisted, Christianity is concerned with *totus homo*, the 'entire human person', not just the human mind.[5] In this, Luther was doing nothing more than stressing the importance of maintaining a biblical understanding of human nature in every aspect of Christian living. The

Australian writer Robert Banks points out the implications for spirituality of this biblical view of human nature when he notes that spirituality concerns 'not only our spirit – also our minds, wills, imaginations, feelings and bodies'.[6]

This insight was familiar to the evangelical tradition before the Enlightenment, and it is high time we rediscovered it. For Banks, spirituality is about 'the character and quality of our life with God, among fellow-Christians and in the world'. Banks deliberately avoids two inadequate approaches to spirituality – a purely intellectual or cerebral approach, which engages the mind and nothing else, and a purely 'interiorized' approach, which bears no relation to the realities of everyday life or to the truths of Scripture. We have a lot of lost ground to make up here, but it can be done. We can reclaim our Christian heritage again. The approach adopted in this book is to retrieve evangelical approaches to spirituality that were suppressed by the Enlightenment, but that are of vital importance today.

Understanding and appreciation

There is a tension within evangelicalism between the *intellectual* and *emotional* aspects of faith. Faith is related to both our minds and our experience; it concerns both Word and Spirit. Christians do not just believe; they believe certain things. Yet Christian faith is about far more than understanding ideas: it is about the transformation of our experience and the renewal of our lives. A fully developed Christian spirituality will thus deal with both these aspects, which I propose to refer to as 'understanding' and 'appreciation'.

'Understanding' concerns grasping the way in which the central ideas of the Christian faith relate to one another. It is about recognizing the coherence of the Christian faith, and gaining confidence in its intellectual credentials. The process of Christian maturity thus involves the use of the *mind* to uncover the way in which Christian doctrines relate to and reinforce one another.

'Appreciation' concerns grasping the way in which the Christian faith changes our outlook on life, and our experience. There is far more to being a Christian than just understanding a few ideas! Appreciation of the gospel involves grasping the way in which the gospel transforms our experience and lives. It involves discovering the emotional aspects of the Christian faith, by recognizing the way in which our experiential world is changed by the good news of Jesus Christ. The process of Christian maturing involves the use of the *imagination* to identify and appreciate the emotional aspects of the gospel, and their implications for Christian living.

The need for guidance

It is obvious that evangelicalism has many strengths,[7] yet it also has its weaknesses. One such weakness is its assumption that people will instinctively know how to read Scripture for all that it is worth. This is simply not true – people need help and guidance. Many young Christians are told to 'read Scripture', so they begin to do so – but soon find themselves puzzled, perplexed, and confused. Their spiritual lives then wither, and their young faith can collapse. This is because they are not being given help. We need to rediscover the great evangelical tradition of the older Christian who will act as mentor to their younger friends. In Christian literature of the early nineteenth century, we find reference to 'letters of spiritual counsel', in which older Christians passed on their wisdom to those who were beginning the life of faith. This tradition of 'spiritual direction' remains of fundamental importance today, and its neglect is inexcusable.

Part of the problem is evangelicalism's natural suspicion of direction and structures, both of which it regards as potentially leading into some form of legalism. This suspicion is well founded, yet it need not be. John Calvin wrote of God 'accommodating himself to our capacity'.[8] In other words, God knows our weaknesses and needs – after all, he did create us! Therefore God makes allowance for our weaknesses in his dealings with us. Evangelicalism has not been very responsive to this point, often failing to recognize that people need structures and guidance, on account of their weaknesses. If structures and guidance are seen as ends in themselves, they are inexcusable. However, they *should* be seen as means to a greater end – the fuller knowledge of God. Thus Christians need practical guidance as to what to *do* if they are to get the most out of the reading of Scripture. It is not enough to be told to read Scripture; we need help with the best possible ways of doing this.

This book provides precisely this practical guidance, by making suggestions as to what you can do. It provides all the information and material you need; it assumes that you do need help, and offers you that help.

But enough has been said by way of introduction – it is time to get on with studying Scripture.

1 BEING LOST

The Christian gospel is like a diamond: not only is it precious, but it has many facets. Imagine someone holding a diamond up to the light, and then slowly rotating it. As each facet of the diamond comes into view, it reflects the light in a sparkling display. Its brilliance is clear for all to see. Likewise, we need to appreciate the brilliance of the gospel, by exploring each of its many aspects. In the various study sessions in this book, we will explore the many facets of the Christian faith. We begin, though, with the theme of 'being lost'.

In order to appreciate the joy and privilege of being a Christian, we first need to imagine what it feels like to be without God. What is it like to be without hope? To be without joy? To be without purpose? To be lost?

Being lost

Suppose you are lost – take a few minutes to focus your mind on this idea. Try to remember a time in your life when you felt lost, lonely, and frightened. Be prepared to share your experiences, to build up a picture of what it means to be lost.

When I was young, I cycled around France with two fellow students during our summer vacation. After a month or so, the time came to return to England. We headed north towards the port of Le Havre, the aim being to board an evening ferry. However, we didn't allow enough time for the journey, and by the early afternoon we realized that we might not get to the port in time. Therefore we decided it would be best to take a short cut. Our dog-eared Michelin map showed that there were some tracks through a great oak forest in Normandy; by going through the forest, rather than round it, we could save time. So we started to cycle down a path that led into this mass of trees.

For the first half hour, all was well, for the track was clearly visible. However, as we pressed on, things started to go wrong. The great canopy of leaves above us began to block out the sunlight, and it became more difficult to see the path ahead, which seemed to split up into a whole series of smaller tracks. The sun faded from view as the dark clouds of a late summer thunderstorm gathered. Eventually, it became impossible to see anything at all. Torrential rain began to pour down through the leaves far above us, and we had no choice but to stay where we were. We did not have the slightest idea where we were. All that we knew was that we were lost in a forest, and would not be able to find our way out until the next morning.

As the three of us sat at the base of an oak tree, getting wetter and more miserable with every minute that passed, we were able to share our feelings. The dominant feeling seemed to be that of helplessness, for there did not seem to be anything we could do. To press on would run the risk of taking a wrong turning, and we would end up being even worse off than we were already. There was an atmosphere of real despair. We knew we would miss the ferry, and not be able to return home as planned. There was also a distinct element of fear. Each of us was aware that we were on our own in a strange country. In reality, we probably were not in danger – but in the darkness it didn't seem that way!

Eventually, dawn came, allowing us to move on. The early morning sunlight lit up the forest track, and also enabled us to gain our bearings from the direction of the light. We headed north, and an hour or so later emerged from the woods. You can imagine how relieved we were! We were able to rearrange our passage on the ferry, and returned to England late the following afternoon.

Most of us have had an experience of being lost. Spend a few moments trying to think yourself into this situation. If you are in a group, you may have been particularly impressed by someone else's description of being lost. Try to think yourself into that situation. This time, though, imagine that it is you who is lost. Use the following prompts to build up your mental picture of what being lost feels like. Spend a few moments focusing on each statement, as you build up your overall impression:

- You are alone in a deep wood.
- It is dark and cold.
- You do not know where you are.
- You have nothing that will give light or heat.
- You are frightened.

When you feel that you have created the atmosphere of despair and fear that is associated with being lost, move on to the next stage:

- In the distance, you see a light moving.
- Initially, you are frightened. Who can it be?
- But then you hear him call your name. *Your* name – not somebody else's.
- It is a kind voice.
- You feel attracted to him.
- You see him draw near. You are no longer frightened.
- He tells you that he has come to take you home.
- You feel that you can trust him.
- He then leads you to safety, food, and warmth.

Try to savour every aspect of this, realizing how your situation would be totally transformed by this person. You could never find your way home by yourself. Yet this person knows you, and is taking you home.

This is a central theme of the Christian faith. Without Christ, we are hopelessly lost in a dark world. We long to find our way home, but have no idea where that home is, or how to get there. But in his great love for us, God sent his Son Jesus Christ to bring us home. Yet Christ does not just *show* us the way – through his cross and resurrection, he opens up a road to heaven that was not there before. And he does not simply point to that road, and tell us to walk down it. Instead, he makes the journey with us, reassuring and comforting us as we travel, just as he thrilled those who once walked on the road to Emmaus all those years ago (Luke 24.13–32). Jesus does not just show us the way to heaven. He established that way. He is that way. And he will travel that way with us.

All of this is beautifully summarized in one of the great 'I am' sayings in John's Gospel:

John 14.6

I am the way and the truth and the life. No-one comes to the Father except through me.

- Savour this verse, and commit it to memory if you do not already know it. What ideas does this verse bring to mind?

Pause

It always helps to compare your ideas with somebody else's. So spend a few moments thinking about what Martin Luther said about this verse, drawing out its enormous spiritual importance:

> Christ alone can and must show us the right way to heaven, and lead us on that way. He is the only one who knows that way, and he himself has travelled on that way before us. He came down from heaven for no other reason than to show us this way, and to take us to heaven through himself. . . . Feel Christ's presence, so that he can say to you, as he did to Thomas here: 'Why are you looking for other ways? Look to me, and set aside all thoughts of any other way to heaven. Think of nothing but these words of mine, "I am the way". So make sure that you tread on me, that is, that you cling to me with a strong faith and great confidence. I will be the bridge which will carry you across. You will pass over from death and the fear of hell into the life which awaits you. For I paved that way and path for you. I walked across it myself, so that I might take you and all my people across. All that you need do is place your feet confidently upon me.'

Study Panel I: Who was Martin Luther?

Martin Luther was one of the great reformers of the Church in the sixteenth century. During the sixteenth century, the Church seemed to many to have lost its way, and to be in urgent need of renewal and reform. Luther was born in north-eastern Germany in 1483. Although he initially wanted to be a lawyer, he eventually decided to go into the Church. In 1512, Luther became a professor of biblical studies at the University of Wittenberg. While lecturing on the text of Scripture, he came to realize that his sins were not forgiven on the basis of his own achievements, but on account of what Christ achieved for him on the cross. The doctrine of 'justification by faith' came to be of central importance to him, as it expressed the crucial truth that God forgives our sin only through Jesus Christ. However, Luther began to realize that the Church as a whole had lost sight of this central doctrine. Thus he began to campaign for the restoration of this doctrine, and others, within the Church.

The great historical movement that is usually known as 'the Reformation' is generally thought to have been triggered by Luther in October 1517, as a result of his protest against the sale of indulgences (pieces of paper, issued on behalf of the Church, that offered forgiveness of sins in return for a payment of money). Luther rapidly rose to prominence as one of many who were campaigning for a return to biblical teaching and ethics within the Church. His campaign was supported by a wide range of writings, including several major biblical commentaries and sermon series. Luther's comments on John 14 in the extract above are taken from his sermons on John's Gospel, which were preached during 1537. Luther died in 1546.

Luther's image of a bridge in the extract is enormously helpful. Many will remember the disaster at the Belgian port of Zeebrugge in 1987. The car ferry called *Herald of Free*

Enterprise had just left port, when something went drastically wrong. The ship's bow doors opened, and water cascaded inside. Quickly, the ferry began to sink, and panic spread among those inside. Tragically, over one hundred and eighty people lost their lives. Yet one story of heroism stood out above all others. One passenger arched himself across a gap in the ship's structures, allowing others to crawl over him, away from the rising water. His body was the bridge that allowed people to pass over from danger to safety. Without this human bridge, even more passengers would have drowned.

Luther asks us to think of Jesus Christ as the bridge between death and life. By clinging securely to him, we can cross over. Christ gave his life in order that we might do this, and have his hope. Without Christ as the bridge from death to life, we would have no grounds for hope. Part of the great joy of the gospel is that God himself has made this hope possible and real. We are lost – yet God has come and found us, and brought us home.

Being in debt

Imagine that you are hopelessly in debt. One of the most powerful of the parables of Jesus is based on people being thrown into prison for failing to pay debts (Matthew 18.23–34). Maybe you have read novels that are set in Victorian London, such as those of Charles Dickens. The theme of debtors being mercilessly hurled into prison is only too common in such stories. In fact, people's lives were often poised on a knife-edge. If they fell into debt, they were at the mercy of their creditors. It was a hopeless situation. Dickens's shocking de-scriptions of these prisons brings out the grim hopelessness of the situation of those within them. Such prisoners were with-out money, and without hope.

● Have you ever been in a situation like that? What is it like to be trapped in a situation of debt? What does it feel like to be without hope in this kind of situation?

| *Pause* |

With that grim picture of a debtors' prison in mind, let us return to the parable told by Jesus to bring out the wonder of forgiveness. The parable makes two points: first, how amazing it is that God forgives us our sins; second, that we ought to forgive others. We shall concentrate our attention on the first point:

Matthew 18.23–7

23Therefore, the kingdom of heaven is like a king who wanted to settle accounts with his servants. 24As he began the settlement, a man who owed him ten thousand talents was brought to him. 25Since he was not able to pay, the master ordered that he and his wife and his children and all that he had be sold to repay the debt. 26The servant fell on his knees before him. 'Be patient with me,' he begged, 'and I will pay back everything.' 27The servant's master took pity on him, cancelled the debt and let him go.

Think yourself into this situation. Perhaps the servant has borrowed very heavily, hoping to make a fortune from some shrewd and highly speculative investments. Yet they came to nothing, and suddenly the king declares that he wants to sort out his affairs. Everyone who owes him anything must pay up – immediately. The servant's world is thrown into chaos. All the calculations are carried out, and the servant is discovered to be seriously in debt. In fact, he is *hopelessly* in debt. He owes the king ten thousand talents – which would be millions of pounds in our currency. And he has no way of repaying him. Not surprisingly, the king is very angry and wants his money back. Therefore he orders that the servant and all of his family should be sold into slavery to repay the debt.

- Imagine that *you* are that servant. How would you feel? What hope would the future hold? What would you expect to happen next?

Pause

Can you see how desperate the servant's situation is? He does not possess the money he needs to repay the debt; and if he and his entire family are sold into slavery, they will live in misery for the rest of their lives. The servant's foolishness has devastating implications for himself and his children, just as Adam's sin has implications for us. There is no way in which the servant can get himself out of his mess. Concentrate in your thoughts on the plight of the servant, and realize how powerless and hopeless he is in this situation. He longs to be able to pay off the debt, and secure his own future and that of his wife and children. Yet he cannot do anything.

Anything, that is, except make a desperate appeal to the king. But why should the king write off a debt of millions? The servant offers to pay back the debt, but this is just wishful thinking. Everyone watching this pathetic little scene would know that there was no way he could make the repayment. Then suddenly the unexpected happens. We tend not to think of it as being unexpected, because we are so familiar with this parable, and the theme of God's graciousness. But the next statement would have come like a thunderbolt to Peter, as he heard Jesus tell this parable for the first time. *The king cancels the debt.* The most that anyone might dare to expect is that the king would agree to some kind of long-term repayment. But instead, the debt is written off completely. There certainly would have been gasps of amazement from those hearing the king's words.

- How do you think people would have reacted to this parable when they first heard it from the lips of Jesus?

Pause

We have got used to God forgiving people. As one cynical Frenchman once said: 'Of course God will forgive sins. That's his job.' Yet we need to rediscover the wonder of forgiveness. Why? There are two main reasons:

1 We will never appreciate the enormous privilege of being forgiven until we realize how amazing a thing forgiveness is! 2 We will not be able to convey the excitement and wonder of the gospel effectively to our friends and neighbours unless we have experienced that excitement and wonder for ourselves.

• The New Testament declares that we are all sinners, and that everyone who is born into the world is held captive by sin. But what does that word 'sin' mean to us? How would you explain this major biblical theme to a non-Christian friend?

Pause

Sin can be thought of in several ways. We began to explore some of these ways in the last section of the study – for example, sin as 'lostness' and 'debt'. Sin is a complex idea, just as redemption is also a complex and rich notion. To begin with, we shall build up a picture of the many aspects of sin:

1 Sin is moral guilt, which must be forgiven before we can have access to God.
2 Sin is uncleanliness. We are stained by sin, and need to be washed and cleansed before we can come into the presence of God.
3 Sin is rebellion against God, in which we choose to go our own way, and disregard his advice and guidance.
4 Sin is like an illness, such as blindness or deafness, which prevents us from knowing the truth about God. We need to be healed before we can come to God.
5 Sin is falling short of what God requires and expects of us.
6 Sin is a force that imprisons us and limits our freedom.

This final aspect of sin is worth further thought.

Being trapped

An image that has often been used in Christian thinking about the sinful human situation is that of being trapped. The Old Testament refers to the fear of being trapped in a net or a pit. Let us take this image, and explore its potential for helping us understand and appreciate the gospel message. We will focus on the central themes of 'lostness' and 'grace'. Build up a mental picture of your situation, using what follows to stimulate your thoughts:

- Imagine that you have fallen into a pit. Perhaps it is a disused well, or an old mine shaft that people have forgotten about.
- You try desperately to climb out, but the walls are steep and slippery. You keep falling back into the pit. You become tired, and hurt yourself through attempting to clamber out. Eventually, you are forced to stop trying.
- It is dark and cold.
- Nobody knows that you are there.
- You shout for help, but nobody hears.
- You are frightened and anxious.
- Eventually, you huddle up against the side of the pit, and try to keep yourself warm.

After what seems like a very long time, someone comes along. He notices you, but he doesn't seem to be very sympathetic. 'Why don't you climb out?' he asks. 'Pull yourself together – stop being a fool, and get out.' When you fail to get out, he walks off in disgust.

The simple point here is that we cannot save ourselves. In our earlier example, we saw how we do not have the resources to pay off our debts. In the same way, we are not capable of getting ourselves out of our sinful situations by ourselves. It is like being in a prison cell. We cannot get out by ourselves; we need help. We do not need religious teachers; we need a saviour – someone who will rescue us. And that is what 'grace' is all about.

Now imagine someone else coming along. He sees that you are in difficulty, and knows that you cannot get out. Now see him climbing down into the pit. He comes to where you are! Then he gently lifts you up, and carries you to safety. He rescues you from the pit.

Can you see the implications of this analogy? Spend a few more moments savouring it, then consider what the analogy is pointing to. It reminds us that Jesus Christ came into this world to be our Saviour. He chose to share our human condition and our human situation. We'll explore this theme in more detail in our next study.

Here is a short definition of grace:

Grace is God giving us things that we do not deserve,
and shielding us from things that we do deserve.

This neat definition is very helpful. It draws our attention to the fact that God does not give us what we really deserve (such as death and condemnation), but instead gives us gifts to which we really have no right or claim at all – such as eternal life, access to God's presence, and forgiveness of our sins.

We matter to God

Up to this point, we've been thinking about our delight and joy about being found and forgiven, but the gospel adds another element to this picture. It declares that God himself is over-joyed at having found us. This is brought out with great clarity in the three parables about 'lostness' brought together in the fifteenth chapter of Luke's Gospel. In what follows, we will explore each of them. The three parables are told to a specific group of people, who Luke identifies as 'the Pharisees and the teachers of the law' (Luke 15.2), who were annoyed that Jesus was talking to people who they regarded as unworthy and wretched.

Study Panel 2: Luke's Gospel

Luke's Gospel is the third of the four Gospels. It is the first part of a two-part work, the second being the Acts of the Apostles. Taken together, these two works constitute the longest piece of writing in the New Testament. Both works are dedicated to a man named Theophilus (literally meaning 'a lover of God'), who may well have been a wealthy and influential Christian sympathizer at Rome. It is not clear when Luke's Gospel was written. The abrupt ending of the account of Paul's imprisonment in the Acts of the Apostles suggests an early date for the two-part work, such as some time in the period AD 59–63. However, many scholars argue that Luke draws upon Mark's Gospel at points, suggesting that the third Gospel is to be dated later than the second, and pointing to the AD 70s as a possible date for the compilation of this Gospel.

Luke himself was probably a Gentile (that is, someone who was not Jewish) by birth, with an outstanding command of written Greek. He was a physician, and the travelling companion of Paul at various points during his career. Luke's Gospel has clearly been written with the interests and needs of non-Jewish readers in mind, apparently with a special concern of bringing out the relevance of the 'good news' for the poor, lost, oppressed, and needy. This contrasts with Matthew's Gospel, which has a clear interest in showing the relevance of Jesus Christ for the Jewish people. Matthew thus takes considerable care to bring out the way in which Jesus Christ fulfils the Old Testament laws and prophecies. Luke, however, explains and illustrates the significance of Jesus Christ in terms that make sense to those who are not Jewish, or do not have a deep knowledge of the Old Testament. Luke is able to bring out the way in which Jesus Christ rescues those who are lost in terms that continue to make sense today. The three parables of Jesus Christ that are brought together in Luke 15 are superb illustrations of the relevance of the good news to people who are lost, even if they have yet to fully appreciate this fact.

> **Luke 15.4–7**
> 4Suppose one of you has a hundred sheep and loses one
> of them. Does he not leave the ninety-nine in the open
> country and go after the lost sheep until he finds it? 5And
> when he finds it, he joyfully puts it on his shoulders 6and
> goes home. Then he calls his friends and neighbours to-
> gether and says, 'Rejoice with me; I have found my lost
> sheep.' 7I tell you that in the same way there will be more
> rejoicing in heaven over one sinner who repents than over
> ninety-nine righteous persons who do not need to repent.

This parable captures the imagination of shepherds, but it can
just as easily be related to our own experience. Re-read the passage, then spend a few moments focusing on the following points:

1 The sheep *matters* to the shepherd. He is prepared to spend
time searching for it, even though he already has other sheep.
2 When the shepherd finds it, he does not order it to return
home; nor does he drag it back. *He carries it on his shoulders.*
Notice the tender and loving way in which he treats the animal. It may have been exhausted, and even injured, through its
wanderings. The shepherd is so delighted to have it restored to
him that he thinks nothing of the time and trouble he must take
to bring it home.
3 The shepherd is delighted to have his sheep restored, and
shares that joy with his friends and neighbours.

> **Luke 15.8–10**
> 8Or suppose a woman has ten silver coins and loses one.
> Does she not light a lamp, sweep the house and search
> carefully until she finds it? 9And when she finds it, she calls
> her friends and neighbours together and says, 'Rejoice
> with me; I have found my lost coin.' 10In the same way, I
> tell you, there is rejoicing in the presence of the angels of
> God over one sinner who repents.

This parable makes its appeal to the world of experience of women at home, but it can just as easily be related to our own experience. Notice how the same themes recur: something has been lost; it matters; it is worth finding, no matter how long it takes. And when it is found, it is a cause for rejoicing.

● Have you lost something, and given up hope that it would ever be found? Do you know of anyone who was in this situation, and how they felt when something – or someone – who they had given up for lost was restored to them?

> ## Pause

Luke 15.11–24

¹¹Jesus continued: 'There was a man who had two sons. ¹²The younger one said to his father, "Father, give me my share of the estate." So he divided his property between them. ¹³Not long after that, the younger son got together all he had, set off for a distant country and there squandered his wealth in wild living. ¹⁴After he had spent everything, there was a severe famine in that whole country, and he began to be in need. ¹⁵So he went and hired himself out to a citizen of that country, who sent him to his fields to feed pigs. ¹⁶He longed to fill his stomach with the pods that the pigs were eating, but no-one gave him anything. ¹⁷When he came to his senses, he said, "How many of my father's hired men have food to spare, and here I am starving to death! ¹⁸I will set out and go back to my father and say to him: Father, I have sinned against heaven and against you. ¹⁹I am no longer worthy to be called your son; make me like one of your hired men." ²⁰So he got up and went to his father. But while he was still a long way off, his father saw him and was filled with compassion for him; he ran to his son, threw his arms around him and kissed him. ²¹The son said to him, "Father, I have sinned against heaven and against you. I am no longer worthy to

be called your son." 22But the father said to his servants, "Quick! Bring the best robe and put it on him. Put a ring on his finger and sandals on his feet. 23Bring the fattened calf and kill it. Let's have a feast and celebrate. 24For this son of mine was dead and is alive again; he was lost and is found." So they began to celebrate.'

This parable, which is often referred to as the 'parable of the prodigal son' ('prodigal' means 'wasteful'), is one of the best loved of all the parables. It continues the theme of 'lostness' that was illustrated in the first two parables we looked at. However, it is no longer an animal or coin that is lost; instead, it is a person. Notice especially the following points:

1 The son chooses to leave home. Nobody forced him to; it was his own choice. He reckoned that he would have a better time away from home.

2 The son travels to a 'distant country' to get away from his father. What 'distant countries' do people run away to today? What do they turn to instead of God?

3 After a while, the son realizes that he has made a mistake. He thought that he would be happier and more fulfilled away from home, and that the grass would be greener on the other side of the fence. Yet he was wrong, and he longs to go home. However, he is anxious: would his father ever want to see him again? Many young people who turn away from Christianity, only to discover the dissatisfaction of the world, wonder exactly the same thing. How can they come back?

4 The turning point of the parable is verse 18. Here, the son makes up his mind that he will go home, no matter how humbling it may be. He clearly expects his father to be very angry with him.

5 Notice how the father has been watching and waiting for his son. His delight at his return is overwhelming. Thus we need to explain to our non-Christian friends and neighbours how much God longs to have them turn to him.

6 Notice also how helpful this passage is in relation to our motivation for evangelism. There are many reasons for wanting to share the gospel with others – for one, we are told to! See Matthew 28.19, where the disciples (and, by implication, every Christian) are told to 'go and make disciples of all nations'. And clearly, we want to share the joy of knowing God with those who matter to us. Yet the passages we've just looked at add another vitally important reason to this list: sharing the gospel brings great joy to God.

Sharing the good news of Jesus Christ thus brings joy to those who learn of forgiveness and eternal life, as well as to God himself.

EXERCISES
1 Each of the three parables from Luke's Gospel explains the theme of 'lostness' in terms of situations drawn from everyday life. How would you use situations drawn from your own everyday life to explain and illustrate the theme of 'being lost'?
2 Read the parables in Luke 15 once more. Focus on either the parable of the lost sheep, or the parable of the prodigal son. If you choose the first, write a short story, aimed at children, in which you are the lost sheep. Describe how you became lost, were found, and were carried home. If you choose the second, write up a diary or journal, in which you are the prodigal son, recording your experiences and feelings as you decide to leave home, settle down in the distant land, become miserable, and then return home.

2 BEING RESCUED

In the last study session, we focused on the idea of 'being lost'. The great joy of the gospel is that we have been rescued from this lostness; and it is only when we realize how seriously we are lost that we can appreciate the wonder of having been rescued.

In this second study, we shall consider some of the New Testament images of 'being rescued'. All of them are drawn from everyday life, showing the way in which we can use them to deepen our grasp of our faith. We can deepen that grasp in two different ways:

1 *Understanding*. We can use our minds to reflect on the concepts involved, and gain a deeper understanding of their meaning.

2 *Appreciation*. We can use our imaginations to evoke the situations presupposed by, and emotions associated with, these images, and thus gain a deepened awareness of their importance and relevance.

With these points in mind, we shall try both to understand and appreciate the great biblical theme of redemption in Christ. Redemption is about *being bought by, and belonging to, God.*

Being bought

We begin by thinking about the biblical theme of 'being bought by God' by looking at the terms 'ransom' and 'redemption', two terms that affirm that believers have been liberated from sin by God – albeit at a price.

RANSOM

Jesus himself declared that he came 'to give his life as a ransom for many' (Mark 10.45). This idea is also found at other points in the New Testament; 1 Timothy 2.5–6 speaks of Jesus Christ being a 'mediator between God and men . . . who gave himself as a ransom for all men'. To speak of Jesus' death as a 'ransom' suggests three ideas:

1 It hints at the idea of someone being held in captivity. To many readers of the New Testament, it might evoke the image of some great public figure being held captive, against his or her will. That person's freedom depends totally upon someone being prepared to pay the ransom demand.
2 It points to a price that is paid to bring about the freedom of the captive. The more important the person being held to ransom, the greater the price demanded. One of the most astonishing things about the love of God for us is that he was prepared to pay so dearly to set us free. The price of our freedom was the death of his one and only Son (John 3.16).
3 It points to the great idea of liberation. To ransom someone is to set them free. It is to restore the liberty that Paul speaks of as the 'glorious freedom of the children of God' (Romans 8.21).

To appreciate the importance of all this, think yourself into the situation presupposed by the word 'ransom'. We must never treat any of the biblical images of salvation as mere technical words. They evoke situations – and to appreciate their power and importance, we must enter into that situation, and appreciate the full emotional impact of their natural contexts.

So imagine that you have been thrown into prison. Perhaps you have read newspaper articles or seen television stories about people in this situation. You may think of those Westerners who have been held hostage for many years by Islamic fundamentalists in Lebanon. Or perhaps you have read major works of fiction, such as *The Count of Monte Cristo*, that deal with this theme. Try to imagine being thrown into prison in chains – think yourself into that situation:

- You are trapped in a cold dark room.
- You have been there for a very long time.

- You are in despair. Will you ever see your family and friends again?
- You are frightened. What is going to happen to you?
- There seems to be no hope of release. Who is going to pay for you to be set free? Outside the prison, other people are living their lives as normal; but you are on your own, locked away.

Now imagine you hear a murmured conversation in the corridor outside your cell. You hear the rattling of keys, and suddenly the door of your cell is thrown open. Fresh air and daylight flood in. Your chains are unlocked. You are free to go. Someone has bought your freedom. Can you sense the excitement of this moment? Perhaps you would stagger in disbelief. Is this *really* happening? Try to appreciate your amazement at what is happening. It seems to be too good to be true. Try to imagine how you would feel as:

- You are led outside into the fresh air and daylight.
- The prison door slams shut behind you.
- You look around, warily, only to discover that there is no-body waiting to drag you back inside. You *are* free!
- You see someone coming towards you. It is someone you were once very close to, but have lost touch with.
- They run to greet you. They reassure you: yes, you *are* free! Yes, the ransom price has been paid! *And this person has paid it.*
- Try to imagine your reaction to this person, who has done all this for you. Think of how much you must matter to them. You have gained your freedom – and rediscovered what it means to be loved and valued. How would you feel if this happened to *you?*

> **Pause**

REDEMPTION
Having explored the idea of 'ransom', let us now do the same with the related idea of 'redemption'; the basic idea expressed here is that of 'buying back'.

An example of redemption familiar from the nineteenth and early twentieth century is provided by the pawnbroker. After pawning an item, it is necessary to redeem it – to buy it back from the pawnbroker – in order to re-establish possession of the item. A similar idea underlies the practice of redeeming slaves, a familiar event in New Testament times. A slave could redeem himself by buying his freedom. The word used to describe this event could literally be translated as 'being taken out of the forum (the slave market)'. As with the idea of ransom, we are dealing with the notion of restoring someone to a state of liberty, with the emphasis laid upon liberation, rather than upon the means used to achieve it. The New Testament uses the term in the sense of being 'liberated from captivity' or 'being set free' (Revelation 5.9; 14.3–4).

Imagine that you are a slave. In New Testament times, slavery arose for all sorts of reasons. People might sell themselves into slavery because they were bankrupt. Sometimes people were forced into slavery against their will. Whatever the circumstances, they are trapped in their situation; try to think yourself into that situation. Imagine that you belong to someone else, and that you are condemned to work until you die – unless, that is, someone buys your freedom, or you somehow raise the money to buy your own freedom. But how is that going to happen? Who would value you enough to buy your freedom for you? And where would the money come from? How could anyone afford to set you free? And what is the cost of this redemption? This brings us to our next section.

The cost of being rescued

While thinking about the biblical images of 'ransom' and 'redemption', we looked at the costliness of our salvation. There is a massive price tag on our liberation from enslavement to sin. Paul affirms that Christians are slaves who have been 'bought at a price' (1 Corinthians 6.20; 7.23). The price of our freedom is nothing other than the death of Jesus Christ. Spend a few moments thinking about each of the following verses:

John 3.16

For God so loved the world that he gave his one and only Son, that whoever believes in him shall not perish but have eternal life.

Romans 5.8

God demonstrates his own love for us in this: While we were still sinners, Christ died for us.

Galatians 2.20

I have been crucified with Christ and I no longer live, but Christ lives in me. The life I live in the body, I live by faith in the Son of God, who loved me and gave himself for me.

[In Romans 5.8, it is important to notice that the Greek word translated as 'demonstrates' could also be translated as 'commends' or 'makes abundantly clear'.]

These verses make one point crystal clear: Jesus Christ died so that we might live. The cross is absolutely central to the Christian faith, for here we see the Son of God dying, in order that we (who deserve to die) could go free, and live. To appreciate how moving and humbling this thought should be, let us spend a while reflecting on part of the 'passion narrative' (that is, the account of the suffering and death of Jesus Christ) found in Matthew's Gospel. Read this slowly, then use the points that follow to help you unpack the spiritual richness and depth of this passage:

Matthew 27.33–43

33They came to a place called Golgotha (which means The Place of the Skull). 34There they offered him [Jesus] wine to drink, mixed with gall; but after tasting it, he refused to drink it. 35When they had crucified him, they divided up his clothes by casting lots. 36And sitting down, they kept watch over him there. ³⁷Above his head they placed the written charge against him: THIS IS JESUS, THE KING OF THE JEWS. ³⁸Two robbers were crucified with him, one on his right and one on his left. ³⁹Those who passed by hurled insults at him, shaking their heads ⁴⁰and saying, 'You who are going to destroy the temple and build it in three days, save yourself! Come down from the cross, if you are the Son of God!' ⁴¹In the same way the chief priests, the teachers of the law and the elders mocked him. ⁴²'He saved others,' they said, 'but he can't save himself! He's the king of Israel! Let him come down now from the cross, and we will believe in him. ⁴³He trusts in God. Let God rescue him now if he wants him, for he said, "I am the Son of God." '

• Spend a few moments thinking about this passage. What points particularly stand out for you?

Pause

1 Notice the reference to the soliders dividing up Jesus' clothes by casting lots (verse 35). This represents the fulfilment of the prophecy of the 'righteous sufferer' of Psalm 22 (see especially Psalm 22.18). Many aspects of this Psalm, which speaks of a righteous person suffering at the hands of his persecutors, find their fulfilment in the Gospel passion narratives.

2 Notice the reference to the robbers who were crucified on either side of Jesus Christ. They were guilty of their crimes and, by the standards of their times, deserved to die. Yet in their midst was someone who was righteous. He was not suffering for his own sins, but for the sins of others. In this, we can see a fulfilment of one of the most moving of Old Testament prophecies, usually referred to as the 'suffering servant' (Isaiah 52.13—53.12). This passage is worth reading in itself; however, notice how its reference to the suffering servant being

'numbered with the trangressors' (Isaiah 53.12) finds its fulfil-ment in the crucifixion. Jesus is treated as a transgressor, and placed in their midst at Calvary.

3 Both the crowds around Jesus and their religious leaders mock him. They demand that he should come down off the cross, and save himself. The astonishing thing here is that Jesus chose to remain on the cross, and save us instead. He could have saved himself, but he chose to save us.

The penalty for our sin has been paid by Jesus Christ. Our guilt has been purged by his life-giving and cleansing blood. His death is the only possible and effective expiation for the guilt that the offence of human sin causes a righteous and holy God. This point is made powerfully by Mrs Cecil F. Alexander in her famous hymn 'There Is a Green Hill Far Away':

> There was no other good enough
> To pay the price of sin;
> He only could unlock the gate,
> Of heaven, and let us in.

- What ideas does this verse bring to your mind? How helpful is it in helping you understand the cost of our redemption?

Pause

The price paid by God to achieve our forgiveness is high; his Son died in order that we might be forgiven. Yet the costliness of that forgiveness corresponds to its effectiveness. This is no cut-price deal, which promises much and delivers little. This is a forgiveness that is as real as it is costly, and is made possible and available only through the death of Jesus Christ.

Study Panel 3: Who was Charles Wesley?
Charles Wesley was born in the English village of Epworth in 1707. He was the younger brother of John Wesley, who was born in 1703. At the age of eighteen, Charles went up to

Oxford, where he, John, and two others founded the 'holy club', noted for its emphasis on personal religious discipline. Its members were derisively nicknamed 'the methodists' on account of their emphasis on personal holiness and discipline. In 1735, Charles accompanied his brother to the American colony of Georgia, in an attempt to evangelize the region. He returned the following year, apparently depressed by the fact that he had so little to show for his efforts. Yet although Wesley placed an emphasis on the importance of religious discipline, he seems to have lacked any living personal faith at this time. His was a rather formal form of Christianity. All this changed on 21 May 1738, though, when he underwent some form of conversion experience, in which he 'experienced the witness of adoption'. His brother John had a similar experience three days later, when he 'felt his heart strangely warmed'. Charles now devoted himself to the writing of hymns, in which his new-found faith and enthusiasm could find their full expression. Many of these hymns have become classics, including 'O for a thousand tongues to sing' and 'Love divine, all love excelling'. The hymn that follows was written shortly after his 1738 conversion experience, and was published the following year. Charles Wesley died in 1788.

One of the finest statements of the wonder of redemption is Charles Wesley's hymn entitled 'Free Grace', but best known by the title 'And can it be'. This hymn is here reproduced in its original 1739 version, which includes an important fifth verse – usually omitted in modern versions. The original spelling has been modernized here:

> 1   And can it be that I should gain
>   An interest in the Saviour's blood!
>   Died He for me? – who caused His pain?

For me? – who Him to Death pursued?
Amazing love! How can it be
That Thou, my God, shouldst die for me?

2   'Tis mystery all! the Immortal dies!
    Who can explore His strange Design?
In vain the first-born Seraph tries
    To sound the Depths of Love divine.
'Tis mercy all! Let earth adore;
Let Angel Minds inquire no more.

3   He left His Father's throne above
    (So free, so infinite his grace!)
Emptied Himself of All but Love,
    And bled for Adam's helpless Race.
'Tis Mercy all, immense and free,
For, O my God! it found out Me!

4   Long my imprisoned Spirit lay,
    Fast bound in Sin and Nature's Night
Thine Eye diffused a quickening Ray;
    I woke; the Dungeon flamed with Light.
My chains fell off, my Heart was free,
I rose, went forth, and followed Thee.

5   Still the small inward Voice I hear,
    That whispers all my Sins forgiven;
Still the atoning Blood is near,
    That quenched the Wrath of hostile Heaven:
I feel the Life His Wounds impart;
    I feel my Saviour in my Heart.

6   No Condemnation now I dread,
    Jesus, and all in Him, is mine.
Alive in Him, my Living Head,
    And clothed in Righteousness Divine,
Bold I approach the Eternal Throne,
And claim the Crown, through CHRIST my own.

- This hymn is one of the finest pieces of theological and spiritual writing in the English language. It merits close examination, and can easily become the basis of a deepened personal spirituality. Use the hymn as a gateway to Scripture, noticing how Wesley weaves together a rich variety of central biblical themes to form a spiritual tapestry. What images does Wesley use? And how effective are they in helping us to think about sin and salvation?

Pause

1 Look at the first verse, and notice the central question that Wesley poses. Why would God want anything to do with a sinner like me? Above all, why would he want to *die* for me? This is truly an 'amazing love'. Why should the Saviour die for someone whose sins caused him to go to the cross in the first place? It is a question that all of us have probably asked ourselves at some point. Yet the amazing fact is that he chose to do so. Notice how this theme is also developed in the second and third verses.

2 Now spend some time reading the fourth verse, and absorbing its rich imaginery. Notice how Wesley picks up some of the themes we were exploring earlier. Pick out those themes, one at a time. If you are in a group situation, discuss each of the themes among yourselves. The main one to note is *liberation*; however, there are others. (The word 'quickening' in line 3 means 'bringing to life' or 'lifegiving'.) You may find it helpful to let Wesley's words evoke the image and atmosphere of a dark prison.

3 Now look at the fifth verse. This will be unfamiliar to many readers, as it is not included in later editions of the hymn. However, it is of major importance to understanding Wesley's own spirituality, and the benefits it can bring to its students. The dominant theme here is 'reassurance'.

4 Finally, look at the last verse. This represents a triumphant declaration of the security of the believer in Christ. The believer has come to life in Christ, and is united to him through

faith. As a result, we are able to approach God with confidence, not on account of our own righteousness, but on account of Christ's righteousness, in which we share.

Belonging

A central theme of the gospel is *belonging*. Let us explore this a little, before focusing on one of its major aspects. Let us use the image of a party (the subject of some of the most powerful of the parables (see Matthew 22.2–14 and Luke 14.1–24)) to help our thinking on this matter.

Imagine that it is a cold, wet, and dark night. You are walking along a street. As you walk along, feeling miserable, you notice that you can see into a room in one of the buildings you are passing:

- It looks warm and comfortable.
- Inside, there are people enjoying themselves. They are having a party.
- As you look more closely, you realize that you know some of them.
- They are inside in the warm; you are outside in the cold and wet.
- You wish that you were inside.
- You feel rejected and unwanted.
- You cannot gatecrash the party, for you fear you would be thrown out – and that would only increase your sense of being unwanted and rejected.

It is then that something happens. A door is thrown open, and someone calls out to you: 'Come in! The party isn't complete without you! We want you to be with us! Come and join us!' Imagine how you would feel. You would feel wanted and valued; you would feel a strong sense of belonging. That is what the biblical doctrine of 'election' is all about. It is about being chosen, being invited. It is about God wanting us. There are no unwanted children in God's family; we have been adopted because God wants us.

So what biblical insights should we focus on, as we think about the theme of belonging?

1 We belong to God in the sense that he has made us. We are his possession and his people. Thus Genesis 1.26–7 speaks of us being made in the 'image' or 'likeness' of God. In the ancient world, kings often set up images of themselves throughout their lands in order to assert their authority over them. There is an important reference to this practice in the Book of Daniel, which relates how King Nebuchadnezzar set up a golden image of himself at Babylon, which he commanded to be worshipped (Daniel 3.1–6). Being made in the image of God is an assertion of God's ultimate authority over his creation, and a reminder that all human beings are ultimately responsible to God.

2 We belong to God, in the sense that we are meant to be with him. 'Belonging' is about having the right to be in someone's presence. 'Belonging to a club' is about the right to be there. 'Belonging to a family' is about the rights, privileges, and responsibilities that being a member of that family involves. To 'belong to God' in this sense is to have access to God.

The opposite of belonging is being rejected and being homeless. To be homeless is to have nowhere to go. To belong is to have a home to come back to – just as the prodigal son, despite his failures, discovered that he had a home to which he could return, and where he belonged. We belong! We matter to someone! We have an identity! These are profoundly important biblical ideas. To appreciate their importance, let us consider an important biblical passage that focuses on the theme of 'belonging':

Hosea 1.2–10

2When the LORD began to speak through Hosea, the LORD said to him, 'Go, take to yourself an adulterous wife and children of unfaithfulness, because the land is guilty of the vilest adultery in departing from the LORD.' ³So he married Gomer daughter of Diblaim, and she conceived and bore him a son. ⁴Then the LORD said to Hosea, 'Call him Jezreel, because I will soon punish the house of Jehu for the massacre at Jezreel, and I will put an end to the kingdom of Israel. ⁵In that day I will break Israel's bow in the Valley of Jezreel.' ⁶Gomer conceived again and gave birth to a daughter. Then the LORD said to Hosea, 'Call her Lo-Ruhamah, for I will no longer show love to the house of Israel, that I should at all forgive them. ⁷Yet I will show love to the house of Judah; and I will save them – not by bow, sword or battle, or by horses and horsemen, but by the LORD their God.' ⁸After she had weaned Lo-Ruhamah, Gomer had another son. ⁹Then the LORD said, 'Call him Lo-Ammi, for you are not my people, and I am not your God. ¹⁰Yet the Israelites will be like the sand on the seashore, which cannot be measured or counted. In the place where it was said to them, "You are not my people", they will be called "sons of the living God".'

This is a powerful passage, which dates from a dark period in Israel's history. It seemed as if Israel had rejected the Lord totally, and abandoned him for foreign gods. The prophet Hosea was sent to call Israel back to the Lord. As the passage relates, Hosea married a faithless wife, partly to symbolize the Lord's faithfulness to Israel, despite Israel's faithlessness to the Lord. The names that Hosea was asked to give to the children of this marriage are deeply revealing. The names of the second and third children are particularly important:

1 Lo-Ruhamah (1.6) means 'not loved' or 'not wanted'. Israel has been rejected by the Lord, on account of their faithlessness. He wants nothing more to do with them. He dissociates himself from them. Israel, who was meant to be God's chosen people, has been declared to be 'unwanted'. Can you appreciate the devastating impact of this message of the Lord's rejection of Israel?

2 Lo-Ammi (1.9) means 'not my people'. Once more, the theme of rejection comes to the fore. The convenant relationship between God and his people, which Israel seems to have taken for granted, is declared to be void. Israel has forfeited their right to be called the chosen people of God. They no longer enjoys his love, protection, and presence. Yet notice the promise of *restoration* (1.10). Where they were once rejected, they will later be restored.

● The passage holds out the promise of reconciliation between God and his wayward people. What does this mean for Israel?

$$\boxed{\textbf{Pause}}$$

It means that:

1 Israel will be wanted again.
2 Israel will belong again.

To belong to God is to be able to go home to God; and that is the great privilege of being a Christian believer. It is to have access to God. Most of us hear about the corporate executive who declares 'My door is always open!' In fact, that door usually remains firmly shut. However, Christians have privileged access to the ear and presence of God, on account of all that Christ has done for us.

To explore the importance of 'belonging' in more detail, let us consider another of the great biblical images for 'being rescued'. This is the image of *adoption*. By faith, we are adopted into the family of God (Romans 8.15, 8.23, 9.4; Galatians 4.5; Ephesians 1.5). The image of adoption is used by St Paul to express the distinction between sons of God (believers) and the Son of God (Jesus Christ). It is clear that this is an image drawn from the sphere of Roman family law, with which Paul (and many of his readers) would have been familiar. Under this law, a father was free to adopt individuals from outside his natural family, and give them a legal status of adoption, thus placing them within the family. Although a distinction would still be possible between the natural and adopted children, they have the same legal status. In the eyes of the law, they are all members of the same family, irrespective of their origins.

Paul uses this image to indicate that, through faith, believers come to have the same status as Jesus (as sons of God), without implying that they have the same divine nature as Jesus. Faith brings about a change in our status before God, incorporating us within the family of God, despite the fact that we do not share the same divine origins as Christ. Coming to faith in Christ thus brings about a change in our status. We are adopted into the family of God, with all the benefits that this brings.

So what are these benefits? Two benefits may be singled out as being especially important:

1 To be a member of the family of God is to be an *heir of God*. Paul argues this point as follows. If we are adopted as children of God, we share the same inheritance rights as the natural child. We are thus 'heirs of God' and 'co-heirs with Christ' (Romans 8.17), in that we share in the same inheritance rights as him. This means that, just as Christ suffered and was glorified, so believers may expect to do the same. All that Christ has inherited from God will one day be ours as well. For Paul, this insight is of considerable importance in understanding why believers undergo suffering. Christ suffered before he was glorified; believers must expect to do the same. Just as suffering for the sake of the gospel is real, so is the hope of future glory, as we will share in all that Christ has won by his obedience.

2 Adoption into the family of God brings *a new sense of belonging*. Everyone needs to feel that they belong somewhere. Social psychologists have shown the need for a 'secure base', a community or group that gives people a sense of purpose and an awareness of being valued and loved by others. In human terms, this need is usually met by the family unit. For Christians, this real psychological need is met through being

adopted into the family of God. Believers can rest assured that they are valued within this family, and are thus given a sense of self-confidence that enables them to work in, and witness to, the world – the theme of our next study.

An interesting point . . .
Wooddale Church is based in Eden Prairie in Minnesota. The church was concerned to ensure that its relevance to the local community was clearly understood. The neighbourhood was mainly made up of newcomers, people who were hoping to settle down. They wanted to put down roots and belong. Therefore the church decided to adopt a slogan to get across what it could offer. The slogan? 'A place to belong – a place to become'. The slogan was effective, because it helped people realize that their need to belong could be met by the local Christian community.[1] It opened the doors for ministry and evangelism in that community.

DISCUSSION POINTS
How can we make ourselves more aware of the costliness of our redemption? What can we do to deepen our appreciation of the high cost of our redemption? And how will this help us as we talk about the gospel to our friends and neighbours? Also, how will it motivate us to be more effective in our Christian lives? Share your insights about these questions.

EXERCISES
1 Photocopy Psalm 22, or copy it out. Read it through carefully, until you feel that you can remember as much of it as possible. Now read one of the Gospel passion narratives – Matthew's is especially recommended (Matthew 27). Now read the passion narrative again, and notice how many parallels there are between the prophecy of Psalm 22 and the crucifixion of Jesus. Mark them on your photocopy.
2 You are a hostage, having been taken prisoner in the Middle East some years ago. Write an account of your abduction and imprisonment, in which you document a feeling of hopelessness and helplessness, and your hopes for release.

3 The following is taken from the *Spiritual Exercises* of Igna-
tius Loyola, and is very helpful as a stimulus to thought and
prayer. You will find it helpful to write down your answers to
the three questions he asks:

> Imagine Christ our Lord present before you on the cross.
> Begin to speak to him, and ask how it is that he, the creator,
> should bend down and become a man, and pass from eter-
> nal life to death here in time, so that he could die for our
> sins.
> I shall also reflect on myself, and ask:
> 'What have I done for Christ?'
> 'What am I doing for Christ?'
> 'What should I do for Christ?'

4 Write a commentary on each of the six verses of Charles
Wesley's humn 'Free Grace' given on pages 48–9, in which
you assess the way in which he reflects on the wonder of
redemption.

3 BEING IN THE WORLD

In this study, we shall focus on being Christians in the world. But what is 'the world'? How are we to understand what 'the world' is, and what our relation to it should be? And, above all, how can we live faithfully as Christians in the world, without becoming 'worldly' and losing our distinctive and vital identity as Christians? The most helpful way to begin is to explore the meaning of the word 'world'.

What is 'the world'?

The term 'world' is used in two senses in the New Testament. It is important to appreciate the difference between them:

1 In its positive sense, it refers to the world as God's creation.
2 In its negative sense, it refers to the world as a force that is opposed to God.

These two senses are related. Although the world is God's creation, it has rebelled against him. What was once good, has now become corrupted; and the world now has the potential to corrupt those within it. This point is important, and we shall explore it in a little more detail.

To begin, spend a few moments reflecting on the following well-known verse:

John 3.16
For God so loved the world that he gave his one and only Son, that whoever believes in him shall not perish but have eternal life.

● What is this verse saying about the world?

Pause

We have here a strong statement of God's love for the world. It is his creation; he brought it into existence. And we, who are God's people, must love that world because it has been brought into existence by God. The theme of 'tending the creation' will always be important to Christian spirituality.

A central theme here is that of *stewardship*. We do not own the world. It is not ours; it has simply been entrusted to us. We are stewards, responsible for the well-being of something that does not belong to us. This theme is clearly stated in the account of creation in the Book of Genesis. Take a few moments to reflect on the following verse:

Genesis 2.15
The LORD God took the man and put him in the Garden of Eden to work it and take care of it.

- What does this verse have to say about our place in the world?

Pause

Can you see that this verse defines our role within God's creation? We have been placed by God within his world, and have been given the responsibility of taking care of it. Yet instead of caring for it, we have ruthlessly exploited it. There is a real and urgent need for us to rediscover our responsibility of being 'earth-keepers'. This corresponds to the positive aspects of 'the world'. The world is the place in which we live at present, and which we are asked to care for on behalf of the God who created and owns it.

However, we cannot ignore the fact that 'the world' has fallen, and that it is now opposed to God. Let us turn to reflect on Jesus Christ's prayer for his disciples, as he prepares to leave them to die on the cross. Although the disciples must remain *in* the world, they are not *of* the world:

John 17.14–16

¹⁴I have given them your word and the world has hated them, for they are not of the world any more than I am of the world. ¹⁵My prayer is not that you take them out of the world but that you protect them from the evil one. ¹⁶They are not of the world, even as I am not of it.

- Read these verses through several times, and notice what is being said about the relation of Christians and the world. How would you explain what is being said?

Pause

The main points to note are the following, although you may notice several other issues as well:

1 Just as Jesus Christ is not 'of the world', so Christians must realize that they are in the same position. Jesus Christ makes possible and available a new life and a new hope, which contradicts everything the world stands for. As a result, the world hates him – and will hate Christians as well.

2 Jesus Christ does not pray that God will take believers out of the world. Rather, he asks that they might be supported and protected while they remain in it. Christians are meant to be in the world, even though it is a hostile and dangerous place. The love of God draws us out of the world, but then it sends us back into it.

Being in exile

It helps to have a framework to make sense of our situation. How are we to make sense of this talk about 'being in the world but not of the world'? One way of thinking about this has been very influential in Christian thinking. This is the image of *being in exile.*

Exile was only too familiar to people in Old Testament times. As the great empires of the period expanded their influence, they had to develop ways of coping with the populations of the nations they had defeated or occupied. A favoured method was deportation of populations. In 722 BC, the northern kingdom of Israel was finally conquered by the Assyrians. Israel was to the west of Assyria; and much of the population of the region was deported to the far eastern regions of the empire. They never saw their homeland again. In their place in Israel, the Assyrians settled peoples from elsewhere in their vast empire. These peoples brought their religious beliefs and practices with them to this region, which now came to be known as 'Samaria'. The long-standing tension between Jews and Samaritans has its origins in this development.

The southern kingdom of Judah escaped destruction at the hands of the Assyrians. Yet it too was invaded and defeated, this time by the Babylonians. In 586 BC, the city of Jerusalem finally fell, and much of its population was taken off to exile in Babylon. Imagine how they must have felt. Suppose that the following sequence of events happened to you. How would you feel about it?

● Your city was occupied by foreigners, and all its most important and sacred sites were destroyed.
● You were forced to leave your home, and travel far away, and forced to live in a strange city in a strange country, among people who spoke a language you did not understand, and treated you with contempt.

● How would you feel if you were placed in this situation? How would you cope with 'living in exile'?

Pause

Here are some thoughts that would keep you going in this situation:

1 You would keep alive the hope of returning home, and starting life all over again.

2 You would try to keep alive memories of the homeland.

3 You would know that your true home was elsewhere.

The exiles longed to return to their homeland. One of the most powerful pieces of writing from this period is Psalm 137, which speaks of the thoughts of the exiles as they sat by the 'rivers of Babylon' (a reference to the Tigris and Euphrates, and the canals that were connected to them). Read this Psalm slowly, and notice the sadness it expresses:

Psalm 137.1–6

¹By the rivers of Babylon we sat and wept when we remembered Zion.

²There on the poplars we hung our harps,

³for there our captors asked us for songs,

   our tormentors demanded songs of joy;

   they said, 'Sing us one of the songs of Zion!'

⁴How can we sing the songs of the LORD while in a foreign land?

⁵If I forget you, O Jerusalem, may my right hand forget its skill.

⁶May my tongue cling to the roof of my mouth if I do not remember you,

   if I do not consider Jerusalem my highest joy.

Jerusalem was exiled in Babylon, and looked forward to its return to the homeland. Although living in the great city of Babylon, Jerusalem knew that it did not belong there. To live somewhere does not mean that it is our homeland. It may mean that we are waiting to return home. Christians are in exile on earth. They are in the world, but they look forward to going home. They are citizens of heaven, who are exiled on earth.

The famous North American writer Jonathan Edwards summed up the kind of attitude that Christians ought to have towards the world:

> Though surrounded with outward enjoyments, and settled in families with desirable friends and relations; though we have companions whose society is delightful, and children in whom we see many promising qualifications; though we live by good neighbors and are generally beloved where known; yet we ought not to take our rest in these things as our portion. . . . We ought to possess, enjoy and use them, with no other view but readily to quit them, whenever we are called to it, and to change them willingly for heaven.

Study Panel 4: Who was Jonathan Edwards?
Jonathan Edwards was born in 1703 in Massachussetts. He went to study at Yale College, New Haven (now Yale University); and after a period of studying theology, he underwent a conversion experience, in which 'there came into my soul, and was diffused throughout it, a sense of the glory of the Divine Being'. After a brief period of pastoral ministry in New York, followed by several years of teaching at Yale, Edwards returned to Massachussetts, becoming pastor of a church in Northampton in 1726. Throughout his life, Edwards had a deep sense of obligation to preach the 'glory of the Lord'. In 1734, his preaching led to the outbreak of what is now known as the 'Great Awakening', a period of spiritual renewal and revitalization in the region which had a considerable impact on American Christianity. It was a time of great excitement, as wave after wave of fresh conversions swept through the region. Edwards's account of events during this period remains a spiritual classic. In 1750, he was obliged to leave his church on account of a disagreement about baptism. After a period in the frontier town of Stockbridge, he was called to be the president of Princeton

College, New Jersey (now Princeton University). He was inoculated against smallpox within weeks of taking up this position in March 1758. However, the inoculation was ineffective, and Edwards died several days later.

St Paul also offers a way of understanding our place as Christians in the world. This is found in his letter to the Philippians. Paul's letter to the church at Philippi is generally thought to have been written during a period of imprisonment, probably in Rome, around AD 61. The circumstances of the letter fit in well with those described in Acts 28.14–31, when Paul was under house arrest, but was still permitted to see visitors and enjoy at least some degree of freedom. Philippi was an important Roman colony in Macedonia, and was evangelized by Paul during his second missionary journey (Acts 16.11–40). It was the first European city in which Paul proclaimed the gospel. There were so few Jews in the region that there was no synagogue (Acts 16.16 refers only to a 'place of prayer', not a synagogue). This may explain both why Paul does not cite the Old Testament at all during this letter, and also why the letter is virtually free of argument. It is one of the most positive and delightful of Paul's letters, which sets out the sheer joy of the gospel to its readers.

Paul uses the fact that Philippi was a Roman colony to develop a framework for making sense of the place of the Christian in the world. He sets out this framework very succinctly as follows:

Philippians 3.20
But our citizenship is in heaven. And we eagerly await a Saviour from there, the Lord Jesus Christ.

- What does Paul mean by this?

Pause

To appreciate the implications of this helpful image, let us discover some more about the city of Philippi, to which Paul wrote this much-loved letter. Although Philippi was originally founded as a Greek city, it was later refounded as a Roman colony. The city thus developed a decidedly Roman atmosphere, on account of both the permanent presence of Roman settlers, and the large numbers of Roman troops regularly passing through the city because of its strategic location in Macedonia. The Romans in Philippi were therefore very aware of their links with Rome, including its language (Latin was more widely spoken than Greek) and laws.

The language, imagery, and outlooks of a Roman colony would thus be very familiar to Paul's readers in the city. Paul uses the image of 'citizenship in heaven' to bring out several leading aspects of Christian living in the world, including the following:

1 The Christian Church is an outpost of heaven in a foreign land.
2 It speaks the language of that homeland, and is governed by its laws – despite the fact that the world around it speaks a different language, and obeys a different set of laws.
3 Its institutions are based on those of its homeland.
4 One day, its citizens will return to that homeland, to take up all the privileges and rights which that citizenship confers. This image thus lends dignity and new depths of meaning to the Christian life, especially the tension between the 'now' and 'not yet', and the feeling of being outsiders to a culture, being 'in the world' and yet not 'of the world'.

There are many points of importance in what has just been said, but let us focus on just one of them – the tension between the 'now' and the 'not yet'. We will take Paul's approach one step at a time, and see how helpful it is:

1 Paul does not speak of 'citizenship in heaven' as something that is *future*. It is not something that we have to wait for; we possess it now. Even as we live in this world, we can know that we are citizens of heaven.

2 Citizenship is about rights, privileges, and responsibilities. In the ancient world, it is about the right to live permanently within a city, to share in the privileges and responsibilities which that brings. Those privileges could be considerable: Paul was a Roman citizen, and had no hesitation in claiming the privileges this entailed when he needed to (see Acts 22.25–8).

3 To be a citizen of heaven means that, even though we live on earth, we have the right to live in heaven. We shall return there one day, not as visitors, nor as unwelcome intruders, but as people who have the *right* to be there, and to share in all its joys.

4 Being a citizen of heaven thus holds together the present and the future. We can live in the present knowing that our future is secure. It is like Israel, preparing to enter the promised land. The wanderings in the wilderness were over, and the promised land lay ahead on the other side of the Jordan. The hope of entering that land in the future dominated the thoughts of Israel in the present. We are presently in another country, yet our right of return to our homeland is assured. We can live in the present, knowing that the future is secure. The Christian has a foot in both the world and in heaven. Although we live in the world, we do not share its fallen standards or its hopes. Our hope is fixed on heaven, which changes the way in which we think and live in this world, a point to which we shall return in our final study. We are not in heaven yet, but the sure hope of being there in the future keeps us going and growing as we live in this world.

A natural way of developing Paul's thinking here is to think of Christian churches or congregations as 'colonies of heaven'. With this image in mind, we may consider the role of Christian fellowship in supporting and nourishing the Christian life.

Being in the world

We have already used two images to help us make sense of being a Christian in the world. These were:

1 Being in exile.
2 Living in a colony of heaven.

We are now going to add a third image, which many people find helpful in thinking about their place in the world. This is:

3 Living in an occupied country.

In 1942, C.S. Lewis described Christian faith as existing on 'enemy territory'. Lewis was writing in the midst of the Second World War, when much of continental Europe was occupied by Nazi armies. He was trying to express the idea that faith was like a resistance movement that was hostile to the invading power, and that invading power was determined to stamp out any resistance that it met. Christianity is like a resistance movement, determined to oppose this invading power, and work towards the restoration of the world to its rightful owner. This theme dominates C.S. Lewis's *Narnia* chronicles.

Since 1942, things have changed a lot. In some ways, Western culture has become more open towards the spiritual aspects of life, as the growth of the New Age movement has shown. In other respects, though, it has become more hostile towards the Christian faith. Christian values and presuppositions seem to be in the process of gradually being squeezed out of every area of modern Western culture. Faith, like a resistance movement, has to survive in a very hostile environment. But it *can* survive – in fact, it can do a lot more than that: it can flourish. However, it needs discipline, dedication, and support.

Try to think yourself into the situation faced by the first Christians during the New Testament period. In particular, think about the following points:

1 People treated them with contempt. They were faced with hostility on every side, and were ridiculed as fools. A very early anti-Christian cartoon shows a man kneeling, worshipping a crucified man – with the head of an ass. That's what cultured Romans thought about Christianity!
2 There were not many Christians in those days. In the early stages of their history, Christians were very few in number.

And there were enormous barriers of culture and language to overcome if the gospel was to be spread.

Try to think yourself into these early Christians' situation, and imagine how incredibly despondent you might feel about it. Yet the first Christians were not unduly worried by these problems; they were not overwhelmed by the hostility of their environment. The resurrection of Jesus set those difficulties in perspective. The God who raised Jesus from the dead was with them, and on their side. And neither should we feel intimidated or threatened. In fact, the new hostility of secular culture to the gospel makes it easier for us to identify with the Christian communities we read about in the New Testament letters. In many respects, their situation was very like ours. So take comfort from the experience of the early Christians, and let yourself be inspired and encouraged by their words and examples. Like them, you have the privilege of being a citizen of heaven, and part of that privilege is being able to meet together with your fellow-citizens. You can be with people who share your faith and hope, and sing the praises of the Lord in a strange land.

Christians live, work, and witness in the world. In fact, one of the most important functions of Christian spirituality is to enable believers to live effectively in the world, while maintaining their distinctiveness. To be a Christian is to be *different*. Let us conclude this study by exploring this idea of 'being different'.

Being different

What does it mean to 'exist'? In one sense, the answer is obvious: it means to be there. However, the word has a deeper meaning, which has largely been forgotten. It means 'to stand out'. Christians are those who exist in the world – meaning that they live in the world, but at the same time stand out from it.

This theme is developed in one of the most familiar passages from the Sermon on the Mount. Spend a few moments reading this passage and thinking about it:

Matthew 5.13–16

¹³You are the salt of the earth. But if the salt loses its saltiness, how can it be made salty again? It is no longer good for anything, except to be thrown out and trampled by men. ¹⁴You are the light of the world. A city on a hill cannot be hidden. ¹⁵Neither do people light a lamp and put it under a bowl. Instead they put it on its stand, and it gives light to everyone in the house. ¹⁶In the same way, let your light shine before men, that they may see your good deeds and praise your Father in heaven.

● First, though, let us focus on the affirmation that believers are the 'salt of the earth' (5.13). What sort of ideas does this image convey? How does it help us to understand what it means to be a Christian in the world?

Pause

There are three main points to make concerning this:

1 It emphasizes that being a Christian makes you different. You stand out. Salt gets noticed – and so must Christians be noticed.

My grandmother was very fond of Victoria sponge cakes, and had perfected the art of making them in her old solid-fuel oven. The final stage in the construction of one of these sponge cakes was shaking icing sugar over the top of the cake. Perhaps she got distracted during this final stage on this one particular afternoon. Anyway, whatever the reason may have been, the afternoon tea party was not a success. The room was full of elderly ladies, drinking large quantities of tea from my grandmother's china teacups. When the sponge cake was brought in, there was a general appreciative murmur and anticipation of its delights. As the old ladies were all impeccably mannered, none would allow themselves to begin to eat until everyone had been served. When the last person had been served, a dozen pieces of cake were lifted into a dozen elderly mouths, as if in response to an unseen signal. The cake did not stay there long, though! There was an explosion of spitting and choking. It transpired that my grandmother had accidentally liberally shaken salt all over the cake – and her guests had certainly noticed!

To be a Christian is to be noticed, because we are different. That can be bad news; it can lead to victimization and persecution, as many Christians in Islamic countries know to their cost. However, it also means that people know who to talk to, if they want to discover the joy and wonder of the gospel.

2 Salt is useful. In the ancient world, salt was widely used as a preservative. In the same way, the gospel is about preserving people from death – not meaning that it prevents them from dying, but that it offers them the hope of eternal life. In the midst of a decaying world, Christians can rest assured that they will be saved and preserved. We are being offered something that will not decay or spoil.

Salt was also used to flavour food. Without salt, much food would be bland and tasteless. Salt brings out the flavour of the food, and makes it more palatable. In the same way, the gospel allows us to appreciate life to its full, a theme to which we shall return in the last of these studies.

3 Salt can lose its saltiness. Some scholars believe that Jesus is here referring specifically to rock salt, in which the salt had been absorbed by a porous mineral. The salt could easily be leached out of the mineral, leaving behind useless particles of rock. To remain useful, salt needs to retain its distinctive character. To be of use to God in his world, Christians need to be in that world, yet remain distinct from it.

- Now let us turn to deal with the image of light. What does it mean to speak of Christians being the 'light of the world'?

> ### *Pause*

The image of a 'city on a hill' refers in particular to its visibility at night, on account of the lights within it:

● To appreciate the importance of 'light', imagine the following situation. You are lost in a wilderness or desert. Perhaps you are in Alaska, Arabia, Nevada, or the Australian outback. You are very thirsty. You need to know where to find help if you are to survive, but you cannot see any sign of civilization. There is nothing to suggest that there are living human beings anywhere near you. Now imagine darkness falling. The stars begin to shine, but they are not going to help you find help. Then suddenly you stop dead in your tracks. Somewhere in the distance, a light has twinkled. It was on the horizon, yet too low to be a star. There it is again! You then realize that it is a light. And where there is a light, there may be a house, or even a township. Noting the direction carefully, you begin to walk towards it. Gradually, the light begins to become brighter and clearer, and what had been little more than a twinkle becomes a steady glow. As you press on, the glow of the light resolves itself into a series of tiny pinpricks of light. You have found a township, a place where you can find warmth, water and other people.

A light leads to safety; it shows us where to go. It means that we are no longer lost, and no longer alone. We are lights, because we can help people come home to God, and find peace, forgiveness, and security with him.

● Now imagine what would have happened if everyone in that township had put shutters on their windows, or somehow covered up their lights. You would not have seen anything. You would still be lost, and you could not have found your way. If people do not know that you are a Christian, you will not be able to lead them home to God. When Jesus Christ asks us to let our light shine, he is asking us to *stand up* and *stand out* for him.

Read Matthew 5.16 again. What is the purpose of being a 'light'? The passage makes the answer perfectly clear: *to get yourself noticed.* Yet this is not some kind of self-publicity campaign! It is about drawing attention to God, not to ourselves. The basic motivation for getting noticed is not to increase our own profiles, but to point people to God.

DISCUSSION POINTS

There is a question that you may want to raise here. In the Sermon on the Mount, Jesus refers to *believers* as the 'light of the world'. Yet in John's Gospel, he refers to *himself* as the 'light of the world' (John 8.12). How can both be true? The answer to this question is important, and needs to be understood.

Think of the relation between the sun and the moon. The sun is a source of light. The moon is a dead and cold world, which produces no light of its own. However, it *can* reflect the light of the sun; and at night, the light of the full moon is good enough to let us see. Jesus Christ is like the sun, and we are like the moon. We reflect his light and his glory. We may not possess the same radiance as Christ, but we can faithfully and effectively reflect him; and in the darkness of the world's night, that light is good enough to see by. It is good enough to lead people home to God. And that is one of our central tasks and privileges in this world: to lead people to the delight and joy of knowing Christ as their Saviour and Lord.

EXERCISE

Many people enjoy tracing their family trees, and many Americans and Australians can trace their families back to European or Asian roots. It is fascinating to find out where you come from.

Every Christian has a family tree of faith. You may never have thought of this, but it is a simple fact of life. You are a Christian because of somebody else. Through the faithfulness of another person, you are a Christian today. Some people come to faith through some kind of conversion experience; others gradually absorb the faith, and cannot really identify any moment when they 'became' Christians. Yet that does not matter. It is your present faith, not your past history, that makes you a Christian! Here are some of the ways in which people come to faith:

1 Through your family, especially your parents. You may have been brought up in a Christian household, and gradually absorbed its atmosphere of faith and trust in God.

2 Through a close friend. This is one of the most common and important means of conversion. The patient witness of someone who matters to you may have helped you discover the joy of the gospel.

3 Through what you heard a preacher or travelling evangelist say. Many people look back to international figures such as Billy Graham, and trace the birth of their faith back to listening to him. Others may have been struck by a sermon preached in their local church, which set them firmly on the road to faith.

4 Through reading a book. Many people, especially in situations where Christianity cannot be preached openly, discover the gospel through reading. The New Testament itself is easily the most important book in this respect. Other books, though, have helped people to come to faith.

- Write down how you came to faith. Which person was instrumental in bringing you to faith?

Now spend some time reflecting on this point. The person who helped you come to faith was, in turn, helped by someone else – although you may never know who. Maybe they told you who it was, and how it happened. And that person, in turn, was helped by someone else. There is a long and unbroken connection between you and the New Testament. Just think! Jesus Christ commanded his disciples to 'go and make disciples of all nations' (Matthew 28.19). And someone there on that occasion preached the gospel to someone else, who preached it to someone else – and so it went on and on, until that chain reached you. Your family tree of faith goes straight back through history to the New Testament. Isn't that an amazing thought?

Here is the challenge that this thought brings, though. Will your family tree of faith end with you? Or will there be others, who in years to come will point to you, and say: 'That is the person who put me on the road to faith'? It is a challenging thought. Will we be the 'salt of the earth' to someone? And if not, what are we going to do about it?

4 BELIEVING AND DOUBTING

We now turn to think about the nature of faith. What does it mean to 'believe'? And how does this relate to 'doubt'? The best way to approach these questions is to begin by thinking about certain English words.

Thinking about words

Look at the two words that follow and jot down the kind of ideas that you associate with each of them:

1 Belief.
2 Faith.

Pause

After giving these words some thought, you may have found that the two words imply different things. The word 'belief' may have made you think of two things:

(a) An idea.
(b) Something that you aren't too sure about.

Belief is about believing that an idea is true, even though you cannot be sure about it. Faith, though, is about trusting – trusting someone who you believe to be entirely reliable and worthy of your trust. We will explore this by imagining a situation in which this aspect of faith comes out clearly.

In an earlier study, I asked you to imagine that you were lost at night. Spend a few moments thinking yourself into that situation, using the following prompts to help you do so:

- You are alone in a deep wood.
- It is dark and cold.
- You don't know where you are or which way to turn.
- There is nothing that will give you light or heat.
- You are frightened.

- You can hear things moving in the trees.
- There are shivers going down your spine.

When you feel that you have fully entered into this situation in your imagination, begin to build what follows into your mental picture:

- You hear a noise in the distance.
- It is coming closer.
- It is a man.
- He sees you, and comes towards you.
- He says to you: 'Come with me! I will lead you to safety.'

What would be the first question that would rush through your mind at that moment? Would it be this:

- Is this man *really* there?

It might well be such a question. Perhaps you are very tired, and you are not sure whether you are dreaming or not. However, most people would *not* be wondering whether the man was actually there or not. They would be asking another question. What would your question be?

Pause

The big question that most people would want to know the answer to is this:

- Can I trust him?

In other words, is this man *worthy* of my trust? If I follow this man, will he lead me to safety? Or will he lead me into a trap?

- The Bible affirms that God is worthy of our trust. In what ways does it do this? How does the Bible help us to realize that God can be trusted?

Pause

The Bible affirms this in a number of ways.

First, it declares that God is trustworthy. Think of statements such as the following: 'The one who calls you is faithful and he will do it' (1 Thessalonians 5.24). The original Greek of this verse is quite interesting. The word 'it' is not present; instead, the sense of the Greek is more along the lines of 'and he will *act*', or 'and he will *achieve*'. Thus it is saying that God will not do anything in particular, but he will do whatever is needed, and do it well.

The coming of Jesus Christ is seen by New Testament writers as the supreme demonstration of the trustworthiness of God. All the great hopes and promises of the Old Testament find their fulfilment in him; and that means that we can put our trust in the great New Testament promises of forgiveness and eternal life – because we know that God will deliver what he promises. Spend a few moments reflecting on the following passage:

---

2 Corinthians 1.20–2

[20]For no matter how many promises God has made, they are 'Yes' in Christ. And so through him the 'Amen' is spoken by us to the glory of God. [21]Now it is God who makes both us and you stand firm in Christ. He anointed us, [22]set his seal of ownership on us, and put his Spirit in our hearts as a deposit, guaranteeing what is to come.

- What does this passage say to you about God's promises?

$$\boxed{\textbf{\textit{Pause}}}$$

The following points are worth noting here:

1 God has made many promises to his people. Can they be trusted? Can he be trusted? Notice St Paul's emphatic answer: Christ is the guarantee of the trustworthiness of the God who makes promises, and the promises that he makes.

2 As a result, we can rest assured in the Christian life. The stability and security of our life of faith is grounded in the reliability of God himself, who 'makes us stand firm in Christ'.

3 Note the emphasis placed upon God sealing his ownership of his people. The Holy Spirit is a 'deposit'. The English word 'deposit' can mean something like 'the residue at the bottom of a container'. That is not Paul's meaning here, which is much closer to the word 'deposit' in financial dealings. A deposit is a sum of money that you pay in order to secure ownership of an item. You will pay more later; the deposit, however, gives you ownership of the item you want. God's gift of the Holy Spirit is a mark both of his *owning* us, and also of his intention to *give us more* in the fullness of time.

Faith is therefore about trusting God and the promises that he makes, and responding to these promises. Martin Luther made this point as follows; spend a few moments thinking about what he said:

> For where there is the Word of the God who makes promises, there must necessarily be the faith of the person who accepts them. So it is clear that the beginning of our salvation is a faith which clings to the Word of the God who makes promises, who, without any effort on our part, in free and unmerited mercy goes before us and offers us the word of his promise. 'He sent forth his word, and thus healed them,' [Psalm 107.20] not: 'He accepted our work, and thus healed us.' The Word of God comes first of all. After it follows faith; after faith, love. Then love does every good work, for it does no wrong, indeed, it is the fulfilling of the law [Romans 13.10]. We can only come to God or deal with him through faith.

Secondly, Scripture provides examples of individuals who placed their trust in God, and the results of this trust in their lives. In the Bible, faith is never about mere ideas; it is about lives that are transformed by placing trust in a trustworthy God. Abraham is an especially important illustration of this point. Spend a few moments reading the following, before trying to think yourself into Abraham's situation:

> **Genesis 15.1–6**
>
> [1]After this, the word of the LORD came to Abram in a vision: 'Do not be afraid, Abram. I am your shield, your very great reward.' [2]But Abram said, 'O Sovereign LORD, what can you give me since I remain childless and the one who will inherit my estate is Eliezer of Damascus?' [3]And Abram said, 'You have given me no children; so a servant in my household will be my heir.' [4]Then the word of the LORD came to him: 'This man will not be your heir, but a son coming from your own body will be your heir.' [5]He took him outside and said, 'Look up at the heavens and count the stars – if indeed you can count them.' Then he said to him, 'So shall your offspring be.' [6]Abram believed the LORD, and he credited it to him as righteousness.

As you think yourself into this situation, bear in mind the fact that Abraham (who is called 'Abram' at this stage in his life) is still childless, and had designated his servant Eliezer (15.2) as his legal heir. Now use the following as prompts to your thinking:

- Imagine how hopeless the situation must have seemed to Abraham and his wife Sarah (who is still called 'Sarai' at this stage). They were getting old, and it must have seemed impossible that they would ever have children of their own. Try to imagine how miserable Abraham must have felt.
- Notice how comforting and affirming God's opening words are. Can you sense how deeply reassuring they would have seemed to Abraham?
- Notice also how Abraham has no difficulty in telling God of his difficulties. God already knows them; nevertheless, Abraham is totally open with God. We can see here someone who feels he is with a person whom he can trust.
- The extent of the trust is then put to the test. God makes two promises to Abraham. First, that he will have a son. Can you

see how Abraham would have been torn between wanting to believe this promise, yet wondering if it really was trustworthy? And second, that Abraham will have countless descendants. This would have been even more difficult to believe – but if it was trustworthy, it would be very exciting indeed. Try to imagine the conflict of emotions within Abraham, as he heard these words spoken. Is it too good to be true?

• The climax is then reached. Abraham decides to trust God, and puts his faith in this astonishing promise (15.6). Faith is thus seen as the natural and proper response to God's promises, which counts as righteousness in the sight of God. And as we read on, we discover the way in which this trust transforms Abraham's life.

• Many people find it helpful to have definitions of terms that they use regularly. The term 'faith' is no exception. How would you explain the idea of 'faith' to someone who is not a Christian?

Pause

Here is the definition of faith put forward by the reformer John Calvin; it is a definition that has found wide acceptance. Spend a few moments thinking about this statement, before moving on to the comments that follow:

> Faith is a steady and certain knowledge of the divine benevolence towards us, which is founded upon the truth of the gracious promise of God in Christ, and is both revealed to our minds and sealed in our hearts by the Holy Spirit.

1 Faith is about knowing certain things about God. Notice that, for Calvin, this knowledge focuses on the benevolence of God.

2 Note how faith is grounded in the promises of God, which Calvin argues are made known and made secure through Jesus Christ.

3 Calvin involves both the head and the heart in faith. In each case, the Holy Spirit applies faith, although in slightly different ways.

4 Notice also how there is a trinitarian structure to Calvin's definition of faith: God, Jesus Christ, and the Holy Spirit are all involved.

Study Panel 5: Who was John Calvin?

John Calvin was born in the French city of Noyon, north-east of Paris, in 1509. He studied at the University of Paris during the 1520s, before going on to study law at the university of Orleans. At some point during the early 1530s, Calvin became converted to the cause of the Reformation. When this became public knowledge, he was obliged to flee from France, eventually settling in the Swiss city of Basle in 1535. While he was there, he wrote a book that defended the basic ideas of evangelical Christianity against its opponents inside France. The book which was first published in 1536, was to prove to be one of the most influential books of the sixteenth century. Its title was *The Institutes of the Christian Religion*. Calvin's definition of faith may be found in the final edition of this work, which was published in 1559.

Calvin is also noted for his work as a reformer. In 1536, Calvin was travelling to the city of Strasbourg. He stopped for the night at the city of Geneva, which had recently decided to commit itself to the cause of the Reformation. They desperately needed someone to give them guidance and instruction. While in the city, Calvin was recognized, and asked to stay on to direct the reformation of the city. He agreed. Other than two years of exile in Strasbourg, Calvin remained there for the rest of his life. Apart from writing major series of biblical commentaries, Calvin spent his time planning to bring the Reformation to his native France. Calvin became ill early in 1564, and died shortly afterwards. He was buried in a common grave; to this day, nobody is sure of the exact location of his grave.

But my faith is so weak

Many people are worried about the strength of their faith – 'If only my faith were stronger!' they say. Yet these anxieties need to be set in their proper context. To make this point, let us imagine two situations, and see what can be learned from them:

- Imagine that you want to talk about something very sensitive and confidential with someone else, and you wonder who might be the right person to talk to. Your thoughts then turn to someone called Peter.
- All your friends tell you that Peter is totally untrustworthy.
- However, *you* feel the need to talk to him, despite these reservations. Therefore you decide that you will believe in him with your whole being. You will put your trust in him, using all the power at your disposal to help yourself believe in him. Thus you go ahead and tell him your secret.
- Next morning, all your friends know about your secret. You are humiliated. Not only has your secret become public knowledge, but you have been betrayed by someone you trusted.
- The point being made here is absolutely clear: you can believe and trust passionately in someone, but that doesn't *make* that person worthy of trust. Have you ever been in this situation? Or do you know someone who believed in another person's trustworthiness when there was no good reason to do so?

Pause

Now let us imagine a different situation:

- Again, you need to confide a secret. Your friends tell you that Michelle is totally trustworthy, but you aren't sure. You find it a little difficult to trust her – especially in the light of what happened last time you trusted anyone!
- However, you decide to give it a try. Even though you are not at all sure about Michelle, you tell her your secret.

- The outcome is that not only does your secret remain secure, but Michelle is able to help you deal with it.

The situation here is totally different. You didn't trust Michelle very much, but she *proved* to be totally trustworthy. So what is the point of these two situations? They make a point that is of fundamental importance to Christian spirituality, as follows:

- It is the trustworthiness of the person you trust that really matters, not the intensity of your faith and trust.

If you can grasp this vital point, you will no longer be so anxious about having a 'weak faith'. You may only have a small faith – but you are dealing with a great God.

Martin Luther made the same point in a helpful passage, which is given below. Read it slowly, and see the same points emerge:

> Even if my faith is weak, I still have exactly the same trea-sure and the same Christ as others. There is no dif-ference. . . . It is like two people, each of whom owns a hundred guldens. One may carry them around in a paper bag, the other in an iron chest. But despite these dif-ferences, they both own the same treasure. Thus the Christ who you and I own is one and the same, irrespective of the strength or weakness of your faith or mine.

1 A gulden is an old German coin. Luther begins by making the point that people place or carry treasure in different con-tainers – in this case, a paper bag or an iron chest.
2 It does not matter what the treasure is contained in; the important thing is that the treasure is there.
3 In the same way, Christ (the treasure that Luther refers to) is present in our lives, whether our faith is weak (like a paper bag) or strong (like an iron chest).

We can develop this point further, and in a very helpful way. We will allow Luther to continue to be our guide at this point, and focus again on the relation between faith and Jesus Christ. In a most helpful passage, Luther argues that faith is like a 'wedding ring', which bonds together Christ and the believer. Read the passage slowly, and try to take in its powerful imagery:

> Faith unites the soul with Christ as a bride is united with her bridegroom. As Paul teaches us, Christ and the soul become one flesh by this mystery [Ephesians 5.31–2]. And if they are one flesh, and if the marriage is for real – indeed, it is the most perfect of all marriages, and human marriages are poor examples of this one true marriage – then it follows that everything that they have is held in common, whether good or evil. So the believer can boast of and glory of whatever Christ possesses, as though it were his or her own; and whatever the believer has, Christ claims as his own. Let us see how this works out, and see how it benefits us. Christ is full of grace, life and salvation. The human soul is full of sin, death and damnation. Now let faith come between them. Sin, death and damnation will be Christ's. And grace, life and salvation will be the believer's.

1 Note how Luther sees a direct parallel between faith and a marriage vow. Both establish a personal relationship between two individuals.
2 Note Luther's emphasis upon the sharing of goods. Draw a diagram showing how the man's goods are shared by the woman, and the woman's by the man, in marriage.
3 Now draw another diagram, identifying the 'goods' that are the possession of the sinner and Christ, and how they are shared as a result of faith.

The problem of doubt

Many Christians worry about doubt, for they feel that it is dishonouring to God. They wonder if it is abnormal, and how they can cope with it. However, doubt will always be part of the Christian life, mainly because all of us long for certainty about things. We long to know that everything that we believe is really true. We long to be able to see the risen Christ, and have our faith confirmed and all our doubts driven away. Yet life is not like this. Sheldon Vanauken, an American writer who was converted at Oxford through the ministry of C.S. Lewis, wrote like this about the dilemma of doubt:

> There is a gap between the probable and the proved. How was I to cross it? If I were to stake my whole life on the risen Christ, I wanted proof. I wanted certainty. I wanted to see him eat a bit of fish. I wanted letters of fire across the sky. I got none of these. And I continued to hang about on the edge of the gap. . . . It was a question of whether I was to accept him – *or reject*. My God! There was a gap *behind* me as well! Perhaps the leap to acceptance was a horrifying gamble – but what of the leap to rejection? There might be no certainty that Christ was God – but, by God, there was no certainty that he was not. This was not to be borne. I could not reject Jesus. There was only one thing to do once I had seen the gap behind me. I turned away from it, and flung myself over the gap towards Jesus.

We must never think that doubt is something new, or something that was unknown in the New Testament. To explore this crucial point, let us consider the reaction of the eleven apostles to the appearance of the risen Christ, as it is described in Matthew's Gospel. Read the passage slowly, then let the following prompts focus your thoughts:

Matthew 28.16–20

[16]Then the eleven disciples went to Galilee, to the mountain where Jesus had told them to go. [17]When they saw him, they worshipped him; but some doubted. [18]Then Jesus came to them and said, 'All authority in heaven and on earth has been given to me. [19]Therefore go and make disciples of all nations, baptising them in the name of the Father and of the Son and of the Holy Spirit, [20]and teaching them to obey everything I have commanded you. And surely I will be with you always, to the very end of the age.'

- Picture this scene in your mind. Imagine the risen Christ appearing! Think how wonderful it must have been!
- Think of the reaction you would expect this to have had on the eleven disciples.
- Now notice what really happened. Some 'worshipped' him – the Greek literally means 'bowed down before him'. They recognized who he was, and were overcome with wonder and adoration. However, some 'doubted' – the Greek literally means 'held back' or 'hesitated'. They were in two minds over things. They were not sure; they needed reassurance.

This is remarkable! What *more* proof did they need, we might wonder! Yet the fact remains that some of the disciples closest to Jesus took some persuading before they accepted that he really had risen from the dead.

In John's Gospel, we find a fuller account of doubts about the resurrection. Although the passage in question is very well known, it needs to be read slowly, and savoured:

John 20.19–29

19On the evening of that first day of the week, when the disciples were together, with the doors locked for fear of the Jews, Jesus came and stood among them and said, 'Peace be with you!' 20After he said this, he showed them his hands and side. The disciples were overjoyed when they saw the Lord. 21Again Jesus said, 'Peace be with you! As the Father has sent me, I am sending you.' 22And with that he breathed on them and said, 'Receive the Holy Spirit. 23If you forgive anyone his sins, they are forgiven; if you do not forgive them, they are not forgiven.' 24Now Thomas (called Didymus), one of the Twelve, was not with the disciples when Jesus came. 25When the other disciples told him that they had seen the Lord, he declared, 'Unless I see the nail marks in his hands and put

> my finger where the nails were, and put my hand into his side, I will not believe it.' [26]A week later his disciples were in the house again, and Thomas was with them. Though the doors were locked, Jesus came and stood among them and said, 'Peace be with you!' [27]Then he said to Thomas, 'Put your finger here; see my hands. Reach out your hand and put it into my side. Stop doubting and believe.' [28]Thomas said to him, 'My Lord and my God!' [29]Then Jesus told him, 'Because you have seen me, you have believed; blessed are those who have not seen and yet have believed.'

- Try to imagine the joy, delight, and surprise of the disciples when Jesus Christ made himself known to them – their joy would have known no limits. Yet to those who were not there to witness the presence of the risen Christ, it would have seemed like wishful thinking – maybe even delusion. It seemed just too good to be true.

- That is the position of Thomas. He adopts a thoroughly common-sense approach. How can this be? If he can be reassured, then he will believe it. But he needs to be persuaded. Just about everyone who has read this account has thought something along the following lines: 'That's how I feel. I need reassurance'. They may feel ashamed of those feelings, but that's the way things are for many of us.

- Note that Jesus knows Thomas's dilemma, and graciously resolves it. However, what is most important of all is Thomas's response (verse 28): 'My Lord and my God!' Thomas does not merely record his belief in the fact of the resurrection; he recognizes its implications. If Jesus has been raised from the dead, then he is none other than God, and is to be worshipped and obeyed.

- Now read Jesus' reply very slowly. Can you see its implications? Jesus *knows* that there will be others like Thomas, who will have their doubts. Thus he reassures *us* through Thomas. Our faith is valid! Even though we have not seen

Jesus in the same physical sense as Thomas, we can nevertheless rest assured that Christ has been raised, and is *our* Lord and *our* God, as well as Thomas's.

Earlier, we looked at Calvin's definition of faith, which stressed the reliability of God's promises and the security that faith brings. Yet Calvin went on to write the following:

> When we stress that faith ought to be certain and secure, we do not have in mind a certainty without doubt, or a security without any anxiety. Rather, we affirm that believers have a perpetual struggle with their own lack of faith, and are far from possessing a peaceful conscience, never interrupted by any disturbance. On the other hand, we want to deny that they may fall out of, or depart from, their confidence in the divine mercy, no matter how much they may be troubled.

Once more, we see the same pattern: a recognition of the weakness, sinfulness, and frailty of human nature. Calvin reassures us that our faith, however weak and faltering, is enough to allow us to take hold of Christ, and remain firmly and securely in his loving care. Note how he explicitly acknowledges the struggle that many believers face – but this does not invalidate their faith. The Christian life is indeed about a struggle – against sin, doubt, and evil. Yet in the midst of this struggle, we must learn to trust that the weakness of our faith in no way corresponds to any weakness on the part of our Saviour, or to his commitment to us.

Faith and feelings

Why do we doubt? One reason is that we rely too much on our feelings. If we feel the presence of God, all is well. If we do not feel his presence, we assume that he is not there, and that our faith is deluded. In an earlier study, we focused on the great hymn by Charles Wesley, entitled 'Free Grace'. Let's go back to its fifth verse, and spend some time thinking about it:

5   Still the small inward Voice I hear,
  That whispers all my Sins forgiven;
Still the atoning Blood is near,
  That quenched the Wrath of hostile Heaven:
I feel the Life His Wounds impart;
  I feel my Saviour in my Heart.

● In this verse, Wesley is talking about 'feeling' the presence
of Jesus as Saviour in our lives, and 'feeling' the new life that
he brings. Many Christians will know exactly what Wesley is
talking about, and you may like to think or talk about this
now. Have you had this experience? Do you know someone who has?

Pause

But what happens if you don't feel this presence? What happens if you don't feel this newness of life within you? Does that
mean you have stopped being a Christian? Certainly not! The
truth of Christianity does not depend on how you feel – it rests
on the total trustworthiness of a promising God, and the believing response of his people. To make this point clear, let us
reflect on a particularly important biblical passage – part of
Psalm 42. Read it slowly and carefully. Try to identify with the
Psalmist, as he pours out his anxieties and hopes to God – a
God that he knows to be present and listening, even though he
does not feel his presence at that moment:

Psalm 42.1–11
[1]As the deer pants for streams of water, so my soul pants
for you, O God.
[2]My soul thirsts for God, for the living God. When can I go
and meet with God?
[3]My tears have been my food day and night, while men
say to me all day long, 'Where is your God?'
[4]These things I remember as I pour out my soul: how I
used to go with the multitude, leading the procession to

the house of God, with shouts of joy and thanksgiving among the festive throng

⁵Why are you downcast, O my soul? Why so disturbed within me? Put your hope in God, for I will yet praise him, my Saviour and

⁶my God. My soul is downcast within me; therefore I will remember you from the land of the Jordan, the heights of Hermon – from Mount Mizar.

⁷Deep calls to deep in the roar of your waterfalls; all your waves and breakers have swept over me.

⁸By day the LORD directs his love, at night his song is with me – a prayer to the God of my life.

⁹I say to God my Rock, 'Why have you forgotten me? Why must I go about mourning, oppressed by the enemy?'

¹⁰My bones suffer mortal agony as my foes taunt me, saying to me all day long, 'Where is your God?'

¹¹Why are you downcast, O my soul? Why so disturbed within me? Put your hope in God, for I will yet praise him, my Saviour and my God.

Think yourself into the Psalmist's situation, using the prompts below to help you:

- Notice how he is very conscious of the absence of any experience of God. He longs for God; he is hungry and thirsty for the presence of his Lord.
- He feels that God has forgotten him. Can you appreciate how rejecting this thought is? He feels that he is totally insignificant and valueless in the sight of God.
- Not only is he aware of the absence of God; his enemies are as well. Notice how they make fun of him. They rub salt into his wounds, mocking him. He is reduced to tears, because he can give them no answer. Can you appreciate how downcast and sad he is? When you feel that you can appreciate the Psalmist's misery and sadness, turn your attention to the ways in which he resolves his situation. Read the

passage again, and note the grounds of comfort that he identifies.

- He remembers his experience of God in the past. The reality of that experience is in no way invalidated by his present spiritual turmoil.
- He refers to God as a 'rock'. God is changeless, and remains faithful and constant.
- He looks forward with eager anticipation to the restoration of his experience of God, and the renewal of his praise of his Saviour and God. He knows that his loss of experience of God is temporary, and looks forward to its restoration with eager anticipation.

It is enormously reassuring for us to realize that an inspired writer of Scripture felt the pain of God's absence in his life. If you share that feeling, learn to share also in the Psalmist's firm hope of restoration and renewal.

EXERCISES

1 You are Abraham. Write down your hopes and fears about the future, basing yourself on what you know of his background. Now explain how these hopes and fears are transformed by the encounter with God, described in Genesis 15.1–6. If you prefer, do the same from the perspective of Sarah, Abraham's childless wife.

2 'For no matter how many promises God has made, they are "Yes" in Christ' (2 Corinthians 1.20). Read the first two chapters of Matthew's Gospel carefully, and note how many times Matthew points out how great Old Testament expectations are fulfilled in the birth and early life of Jesus Christ.

3 You are 'Doubting Thomas', writing a letter to a friend about the remarkable things that have happened in Jerusalem after the death of Jesus Christ. The central part of your letter focuses on the events described in John 20. Describe your reaction to the initial reports of the resurrection, and the final climactic appearance of the risen Christ in your presence.

5 LIVING AND HOPING

We now bring this series of studies to a close by focusing on the themes of 'living' and 'hoping'. One central issue to be considered here is the difference that being a Christian makes to life.

Living life to its fullest

What does it mean to 'live'? For many people, life is just a mechanical repetition of tasks and chores, serving no purpose whatsoever. Life is empty and pointless; it is just humdrum, biological existence, in which we wait for an inevitable death. However, the gospel is about eternal life. So what does that mean? If it just means an infinite extension of the pain and problems of this life, it would seem to make our problems worse rather than better. It would offer us more and more of the same. Yet what more people long for is a transformation of their situation.

This point is made in his own characteristic way by the great nineteenth-century Scottish writer George MacDonald. Although his style of writing may seem very old-fashioned to some, the points he makes are as valid today as they ever were:

> [Jesus Christ] is the Redeemer, the Saviour of men, in all senses. 'Ye will not come to me that ye may have life,' he says.
>
> Did it ever occur to you that the root of all your troubles, if you have any – and I have never known the man or the child that had not some trouble – did it ever occur to you that the root of your trouble is that you had not life enough? It is so.
>
> What do I mean by life? Well, I do not mean what many people do, the going on and on in this kind of consciousness that they are in. I suppose that I have led a life

as happy as most people. Thank God I know what trouble is! But trouble could not kill happiness. I have led a life as happy as most people, I say, but rather than go on with this for ever and ever, as some people would seem to like to do, I would rather drop out of existence at once. God knows that I speak the truth. Rather than live with a small proportion of life I would not live at all, I want more life, immeasurably more life. . . . Some of us, perhaps, are beginning to feel old age just coming to stop the activity for a moment of what we call our brain – God knows what it is. And you feel inclined, perhaps, to ask the question in some of these circumstances, or it may be, when some dear friend has gone out of sight: 'Is life worth living?' And then you think: 'Oh, it is very wicked of me to put such a question'. No, friend, it is not; you had better ask it.

I, for my part, if that were life, should say it is not worth living. But where I find that life is an open hill-side, up which I have got to climb (let the darkness be what it may, or be the storm as loud as it may), because there is a paradise on the top, then I say life is worth living, so well worth living that I set my seal to the will of God in making me. Less than that I would not accept from any hand. Give me the perfect life that God meant to give me, or let me die.

MacDonald here puts his finger unerringly on the crucial point: the only way that we are going to live a life that is worth living is by living the life that God intends for us. God created us. God loves us. God wants to give us all that will lead to our salvation and fulfilment. That means taking care to discover how that life is to be had. And Scripture is crystal clear in this respect: it is only by turning to God that we come to life.

This point is made forcefully by an Old Testament writer, who brings out the meaninglessness of life without God. The only one who gives any meaning to life is God himself:

> **Ecclesiastes 2.22–5**
> 22What does a man get for all the toil and anxious striving with which he labours under the sun? 23All his days his work is pain and grief; even at night his mind does not rest. This too is meaningless. 24A man can do nothing better than to eat and drink and find satisfaction in his work. This too, I see, is from the hand of God, 25for without him, who can eat or find enjoyment?

Life to the full

The *Westminster Shorter Catechism* declares that our chief end – in other words, the most important reason for existing – is to 'glorify God and enjoy him for ever'. This is a superb summary of the responsibilities and privileges of being a Christian. The responsibility? To *glorify* God – for example, in worship and through evangelism. And the privilege? To *enjoy* him for ever. God is the true joy-giver, offering and making possible a new way of life. Eternal life is not about an infinite extension of the problems of everyday life. It is about an entirely new way of living and hoping, which is really begun now, yet reaches its fulfilment in the Kingdom of God. Read the following passage:

> **John 10.7–11**
> 7Therefore Jesus said again, 'I tell you the truth, I am the gate for the sheep. 8All who ever came before me were thieves and robbers, but the sheep did not listen to them. 9I am the gate; whoever enters through me will be saved. He will come in and go out, and find pasture. 10The thief comes only to steal and kill and destroy; I have come that they may have life, and have it to the full. 11I am the good shepherd. The good shepherd lays down his life for the sheep.'

- What ideas does this passage and its rich imagery suggest to you? In particular, you should focus on the two 'I am' sayings:

> I am the gate for the sheep (verse 7);
> I am the good shepherd (verse 11).

What do these images suggest?

> ### *Pause*

1 Jesus as the 'gate for the sheep' is an enormously powerful image. Think of the vast numbers of Europeans who emigrated to the United States in the first three decades of the twentieth century. They left behind them misery, poverty, and hopelessness; ahead of them lay a new life. Yet to be admitted to the United States, they had to pass through the immigration controls on Ellis Island, not far from New York's famous Statue of Liberty. Today, Ellis Island is a museum. The names of all those who were admitted are recorded in its archives, and are on public display. If you are American, it is quite possible that your forebears passed through that hall, or that you know someone whose relatives passed through that gateway.

We can easily recapture the atmosphere of that huge immigration hall from old newsreels and photographs. We can see the long lines of people, waiting fearfully and hopefully. Would they be allowed in? Some were forced to return to Europe on the next boat, but most were allowed to walk out of the gateway into America – and to the life of hope that beckoned. The gateway was an image of a transition to a life of hope. To be forced to remain on this side of it meant despair and hopelessness. Can you picture this kind of scene in your mind?

To speak of Jesus as the 'gate for the sheep' is to recognize that safety, security, and hope lie on the far side of Jesus. We can only get there by passing through him. In our first study, we saw how Jesus is a bridge between despair and hope, death and life. We can now picture him as a gate as well. Through his death and resurrection – and *only* through that death and resurrection – we have access to eternal life and the presence of God.

2 Jesus is also the 'good shepherd', but unlike the hired shepherds of ancient times – who ran away the moment danger threatened – Jesus is totally committed to his flock. The extent of that commitment is shown in his willingness to lay down his life for his sheep. In an earlier study, we focused on the great biblical themes of 'ransom' and 'redemption'. The death of Christ is the price paid for our salvation, and the same idea is expressed here. Jesus cares for us so much that he is prepared to lay down his life for us.

3 Yet now we encounter a new idea, which will be of major importance to us in this final study. Jesus declares that the reason for coming is so that we 'may have life, and have it to the full' (verse 10).

- So what does having 'life to the full' mean? What ideas does this image suggest to you?

Pause

Study Panel 6: The 'I Am' Sayings

One of the most distinctive features of John's Gospel is the 'I am' sayings. In their original Greek, these sayings are grammatically unusual, making them stand out from the rest of the text. (This point is difficult to appreciate for readers not familiar with Greek.) There is a direct similarity between these sayings and the form of words used by God in Exodus 3.14, in which he reveals himself to Moses as 'I am who I am'. There is thus an implicit declaration of divinity on the part of Jesus within each of these sayings.

The seven 'I am' sayings are as follows:

6.35	The Bread of Life
8.12, 9.5	The Light of the World
10.7, 9	The Gate for the Sheep

10.11	The Good Shepherd
11.25	The Resurrection and the Life
14.6	The Way, the Truth, and the Life
15.1, 5	The True Vine

Each of them casts light on the meaning of Jesus Christ and his gospel for the world. We explored one of these sayings – 'I am the way, the truth, and the life' – in the first of our studies. In this study, we shall explore the relevance of the remainder of the sayings to our Christian lives.

So how is this fullness of life to be had? How can we, as Christians, continue to experience that richness of life? In John's Gospel, two particularly important means of safeguarding the fullness of the Christian life are identified. We shall explore them both in detail.

FEEDING ON CHRIST

The first way of safeguarding Christian identity and fulfilment is provided by John's Gospel. Read the following passage slowly, noticing the close relationship between 'feeding on Christ' and 'living for ever':

John 6.47–58

[47]'I tell you the truth, he who believes has everlasting life. [48]I am the bread of life. [49]Your forefathers ate the manna in the desert, yet they died. [50]But here is the bread that comes down from heaven, which a man may eat and not die. [51]I am the living bread that came down from heaven. If a man eats of this bread, he will live for ever. This bread is my flesh, which I will give for the life of the world.' [52]Then the Jews began to argue sharply among themselves, 'How can this man give us his flesh to eat?'

> 53Jesus said to them, 'I tell you the truth, unless you can
> eat the flesh of the Son of Man and drink his blood, you
> have no life in you. 54Whoever eats my flesh and drinks
> my blood has eternal life, and I will raise him up at the last
> day. 55For my flesh is real food and my blood is real drink.
> 56Whoever eats my flesh and drinks my blood remains in
> me, and I in him. 57Just as the living Father sent me and I
> live because of the Father, so the one who feeds on me
> will live because of me. 58This is the bread that came
> down from heaven. Our forefathers ate manna and died,
> but he who feeds on this bread will live for ever.'

● This passage focuses on the theme of Jesus Christ as the
'bread of life'. What ideas does this image suggest? What
does it have to say about the nature of Jesus Christ himself,
and the needs of sinful human beings?

Pause

1 One important idea is that of spiritual hunger. Sin leads to
spiritual emptiness and restlessness, and a sense of dissatisfaction. Many people are aware that they lack something – but
have no idea what this 'something' is, or how they could find
it. The gospel declares that God created us to be his. Our true
fulfilment lies only in loving, and being loved by, God. One
early Christian writer, Augustine of Hippo, put this into words:
'You have made us for yourself, and our hearts are restless
until they find their rest in you.'
2 It is by feeding on Jesus Christ that we have fulfilment and
the hope of eternal life. The image of 'feeding' is important. It
indicates that Jesus must be taken and made part of our lives if
he is to transform us. He must be *interiorized*. Jesus Christ
must never be an external figure, but one who lives and reigns
within us.
3 The costliness of eternal life is made overwhelmingly clear.
Christ comes down from heaven to earth specifically to suffer
and die, so that we might have eternal life.

- A practical question remains, though. In what ways can we 'feed' on Christ? You might like to give this question some thought, and write down your answers.

$$\boxed{\textbf{\textit{Pause}}}$$

1 Worship and praise allow us to focus our thoughts on all that God has done for us in Christ. Praise is about appreciating all that Christ has done for us, and responding in joy and thanksgiving.

2 Reading Scripture, particularly the Gospels, is an excellent way of focusing our thoughts upon Christ. To read the Gospels is to discover the wonder of the person and work of Jesus Christ, and the impact that he had upon people.

3 Christian fellowship, particularly small prayer or study groups, allow Christians to share their experience of Christ, and support each other in living out the gospel in the world.

4 Many Christians find the Lord's Supper, or Communion, a deeply moving way of recalling Christ's death on the cross for our salvation. Eating the bread and drinking the wine bring home the importance of the spiritual feeding on Christ.

Other suggestions could be given; these are simply illustrations of some of the approaches that are available.

ABIDING IN CHRIST

A second image taken from John's Gospel is that of Jesus Christ as a vine. Read the following passage slowly. It will be very familiar to many of you, but try to read it as if for the very first time:

John 15.1–6

[1]'I am the true vine, and my Father is the gardener. [2]He cuts off every branch in me that bears no fruit, while every branch that does bear fruit he trims clean so that it will be even more fruitful. [3]You are already clean because of the word I have spoken to you. [4]Remain in me, and I will remain in

you. No branch can bear fruit by itself; it must remain in the vine. Neither can you bear fruit unless you remain in me. 5I am the vine; you are the branches. If a man remains in me and I in him, he will bear much fruit; apart from me you can do nothing. 6If anyone does not remain in me, he is like a branch that is thrown away and withers; such branches are picked up, thrown into the fire and burned.

- Spend a few moments thinking about this text. Write down any thoughts that it generates.

Pause

1 A major theme in the above reading is that of remaining attached to Christ. Older English translations of this section use the term 'abide' (meaning 'stay' or 'stay close to') to translate the word 'remain'. The basic theme is that Christ is the source of all spiritual nourishment. Just as the branch of a vine can only grow and bear fruit if it remains firmly attached to the vine itself, so we can only hope to grow by remaining attached to Christ.

2 A branch that is broken off from the vine will simply wither and die; it becomes nothing more than a dead piece of wood. As it is no use for anything else, it can only be used for firewood. The reference to being 'thrown into the fire' (verse 6) does not have anything to do with hell – it is simply acknowledging the fact that a dead vine branch is totally useless. For want of anything better, it can be used to keep people warm.

3 Notice the reference to pruning in verse 2. In order to enable fruitful branches to bear even more fruit, God prunes them (verse 2). Pruning is a tribute to the potential of a branch. It is an acknowledgement that it is already fruitful, and a recognition of its even greater capacity to bear fruit in the future. Pruning is not just a mark of favour; it is a mark of expectation and anticipation on the part of the vine owner.

Hope

Without hope, life is unbearable. People need to know that there is something ahead that is worth living for. Alexander Pope said: 'Hope springs eternal from the human breast'. It has to, for without it we could not cope with life. Hopelessness is what drives young people to suicide. They cannot see the point of going on.

Being without hope is a tragedy, but a false hope is a farce. Too often, unscrupulous people have exploited the human need for hope. They have offered them hope for the future; too late, though, the hope in question turns out to be false.

The gospel offers real hope. It is no illusion, and no deception. It is about being able to take hold of a loving and living God in this life, and being held firmly by him, until our relationship with him reaches its culmination in the Kingdom of God. Something is *begun* here and now, and will reach its climax later. For people like Martin Luther and John Calvin, the Christian hope is securely grounded in the total trustworthiness of God. God has promised us eternal life; we may therefore rest assured that we who trust in this promise will receive it. And this hope will get noticed by others! 'Always be prepared to give an answer to everyone who asks you to give the reason for the hope that you have' (1 Peter 3.15).

- But how can we be reassured of this hope? How can we live our lives as men and women with hope in our hearts? Spend a few moments thinking about this question.

Pause

Perhaps one of the most helpful answers to this question is summed up in the words 'looking upwards'. We can explore this by looking at St Paul's letter to the Colossians, which vibrates with the theme of hope. He urges his readers to reassure themselves of their hope, in order to maintain an effective Christian life in the present. Read the following verses slowly, and notice the drift of the argument. To look upwards is to remember where Christ has gone, and to be reassured of where we shall finally be at rest:

Colossians 3.1–4

¹Since, then, you have been raised with Christ, set your hearts on things above, where Christ is seated at the right hand of God. ²Set your minds on things above, not on earthly things. ³For you died, and your life is now hidden with Christ in God. ⁴When Christ, who is your life, appears, then you also will appear with him in glory.

Paul is inviting his readers to avoid the trap of living without hope. By looking upwards, they will be reminded of their final destiny, and be able to see their present problems in an eternal perspective. We who have been raised with Christ will finally be with him in heaven. Our present faith, linked to the total trustworthiness of God, will guarantee our future presence in heaven. We must thus live our lives today in the light of that assurance concerning our future.

This point is so important that it needs further thought. Think yourself into the following situation:

- You are in a dead-end job that you hate.
- You find your boss unbearable.
- You have a dingy little office.
- You get paid very little.

Now suppose someone could look into the future, and see what would happen to you. Think how you would cope with this situation in the light of what they told you. Let us imagine two different situations:

- You are told that you will stay in this job for the rest of your life. There is no hope of promotion or a new job.

  Can you sense how hopeless you would feel? You would do the same job day after day, and each day that passed would simply increase your dissatisfaction and resentment. When you feel that you have appreciated this point, imagine that you are told something rather different:

- In six months' time, you will have a job with excellent prospects of further promotion, a bigger salary, and a caring and interesting boss. You will also have a lovely new office.

   How would you feel now? How would you live out the last few months of your job? How would you view your present situation?

Pause

You would now live in hope. Because you knew that your future was bright and assured, you could probably cope with more or less anything that came your way during your final months in your present job. You would even cope with your boss, knowing that you would soon be leaving.

This should be true about the Christian life as well. Christianity enables us to live in the present in the full assurance that our future is safe and secure with God. We can cope with its problems, pains, and sorrows far better than we otherwise could. We share the same world as our non-Christian friends, but we see it in a very different light. It is like the situation that the English poet Frederick Langbridge (1849–1923) envisages:

> Two men look out through the same bars:
> One sees the mud, and one the stars.

Langbridge asks us to imagine two people in prison, looking out through the same window. Although they share the same vantage point, they nevertheless see very different things. The point that Langbridge is making is that some people see nothing but the rut of everyday life, ending in death, while others raise their eyes to heaven, knowing that their ultimate destiny lies with God. Their situation is identical, but their outlooks are totally different. They see the same things, but from a very different perspective. As Christians, we must make sure that our future hopes allow us to live fully and joyfully in the present. An old English prayer for Ascension Day makes this point clearly:

> Grant, we beseech thee, Almighty God, that like as we do believe thy only-begotten Son Jesus Christ to have ascended into the heavens, so we may also in heart and mind thither ascend, and with him continually dwell, who lives and reigns with thee and the Holy Spirit, one God, world without end, Amen.

In an earlier study, we focused on the idea of being 'citizens of heaven'. Although we are in exile on earth at present, we live in the confident hope and certain expectation of returning home one day. We must live today in the light of that hope.

EXERCISES

The American author J. Randall Nichols once wrote of an experience he had while visiting the Greek island of Corfu:

> Some of the most beautiful music I ever heard was the chanting of Greek peasant women, tears streaming down their lined and hardened faces, in a church on Corfu one Good Friday. I asked someone why they were weeping. 'Because,' he said, 'their Christ is dead.' I have often thought that I will never understand what resurrection means until I can weep like that.

Nichols's point is that we can never appreciate the joy and hope of the resurrection, unless we have been plunged into the sense of hopelessness and helplessness that pervaded that first Good Friday. So let us try and experience the joy of Easter from the standpoint of Calvary.

- You are a disciple of Jesus Christ during his earthly life. Spend some time thinking yourself into this situation, using the following prompts to help you:

- You had heard rumours of this wonderful person, and were intrigued. Who was he? What was he like?

- Imagine the situation in which you first met him, and decided to follow him.
- See in your mind the events of his ministry – healing the sick, teaching the crowds, and sitting at table with those who everyone else regarded as outcasts.
- Try to appreciate the enormous sense of expectation that had built up around him. Here was someone who was going to throw out the Romans; here was someone who was going to change the world. Picture in your mind his triumphant entry into Jerusalem. Can you appreciate the excitement and expectation that built up around him?
- He is then betrayed by one of his closest colleagues, and arrested. Can you appreciate the sense of bewilderment that the disciples seem to have experienced? Even Peter denied him.
- Finally, he is nailed to a cross. Many people were still expecting a miracle to happen, and they hoped that God would intervene. Perhaps they thought that armies of angels would descend and rout the executioners – yet nothing of the sort happened.
- Then Jesus dies. Can you see how this would have meant the end of the hopes of so many people? They seem to have forgotten Jesus' assurance of his resurrection. Can you sense the atmosphere of despair and hopelessness on this occasion? Spend a few moments trying to envisage how devastated the disciples were. It must have seemed that all their hopes were buried along with Jesus in the garden tomb.
- Spend a few moments allowing this sense of despair, hopelessness, and helplessness to sink in.

Pause

- Now your thoughts are rudely interrupted. Reports are coming in: the tomb is empty! What has happened? Has the body of Jesus Christ been stolen? Has there been some kind of mass hysteria? You try to control yourself. You dare not hope that something dramatic has happened, in case those hopes are shattered. But something *does* seem to have happened, but you are not sure what! So you decide to talk things over with a friend, as you walk along a road together.

- Read the following passage. You are Cleopas, one of the two disciples in the extract. Think yourself into the situation. Allow yourself to be surprised, delighted, and overjoyed. To make this easier, the passage has been broken up into segments for you. Pause to try to use your imagination to the full. Remember: you are having difficulty taking in what has happened, and its momentous implications:

Luke 24.13–39

13Now that same day two of them were going to a village called Emmaus, about seven miles from Jerualem. 14They were talking with each other about everything that had happened.

15As they talked and discussed these things with each other, Jesus himself came up and walked along with them; 16but they were kept from recognising him. 17He asked them, 'What are you discussing together as you walk along?' They stood still, their faces downcast. 18One of them, named Cleopas, asked him, 'Are you the only one living in Jerusalem who doesn't know the things that have happened there in these days?' 19'What things?' he asked. 'About Jesus of Nazareth,' they replied. 'He was a prophet, powerful in word and deed before God and all the people. 20The chief priests and our rulers handed him over to be sentenced to death, and they crucified him; 21but we had hoped that he was the one who was going to redeem Israel. And what is more, it is the third day since all this took place. 22In addition, some of our women amazed us. They went to the tomb early this morning 23but didn't find his body. They came and told us that they had seen a vision of angels, who said he was alive. 24Then some of our companions went to the tomb and found it just as the women had said, but him they did not see.'

²⁵He said to them, 'How foolish you are, and how slow of heart to believe all that the prophets have spoken! ²⁶Did not the Christ have to suffer these things and then enter his glory?' ²⁷And beginning with Moses and all the Prophets, he explained to them what was said in all the Scriptures concerning himself.

²⁸As they approached the village to which they were going, Jesus acted as if he were going further. ²⁹But they urged him strongly, 'Stay with us, for it is nearly evening; the day is almost over.' So he went in to stay with them.

³⁰When he was at the table with them, he took bread, gave thanks, broke it and began to give it to them. ³¹Then their eyes were opened and they recognised him, and he disappeared from their sight. ³²They asked each other, 'Were not our hearts burning within us while he talked with us on the road and opened the Scriptures to us?'

³³They got up and returned at once to Jerusalem. There they found the Eleven and those with them, assembled together ³⁴and saying, 'It is true! The Lord has risen and has appeared to Simon.' ³⁵Then the two told what had happened on the way, and how Jesus was recognised by them when he broke the bread.

³⁶While they were still talking about this, Jesus himself stood among them and said to them, 'Peace be with you.' ³⁷They were startled and frightened, thinking they saw a ghost. ³⁸He said to them, 'Why are you troubled, and why do doubts rise in your minds? ³⁹Look at my hands and my feet. It is I myself!'

It is no wonder that the first disciples proved such powerful and persuasive evangelists. They knew what they believed, and they knew who they believed in. Perhaps our faith will never have the same vitality unless we can sense that joy and delight, and until our hearts burn to share the good news of the new life and new hope that the gospel brings. But before we can tell others of this joy, we need to experience it for ourselves.

All the studies in this book have aimed to help you understand and appreciate the wonder of the gospel. They are intended to make you *think* about the gospel, to enhance the quality of your own faith, and allow you to become a more effective witness to the wonder and joy of the good news of Jesus Christ.

NOTES

Introduction

1 R.S. Ellwood, *Alternative Altars: Unconventional and Eastern Spirituality in America* (Chicago: University of Chicago Press, 1979).
2 J.R.W. Stott, *I Believe in Preaching* (London: Hodder & Stoughton, 1982), pp. 202–3.
3 S. Kierkegaard, *Unscientific Postscript* (London: Oxford University Press, 1941), pp. 169–224. Cf. P.L. Holmer, 'Kierkegaard and Religious Propositions', *Journal of Religion* 35 (1955), pp. 135–46.
4 The interested reader may like to dip into A.E. McGrath, *The Intellectual Origins of the European Reformation* (Oxford: Basil Blackwell, 1987), pp. 122–74.
5 G. Ebeling, *Lutherstudien II: Disputatio de homine, Text und Hintergrund* (Tübingen: Mohr, 1977), pp. 31–43.
6 R.M. Banks, 'Home Churches and Spirituality', *Interchange* 40 (1986), p. 15.
7 For some suggestions, see A.E. McGrath, *Evangelicalism and the Future of Christianity* (London: Hodder & Stoughton, 1994).
8 See F.L. Battles, 'God Was Accommodating Himself to Human Capacity', *Interpretation* 31 (1977), pp. 19–38.

2 Being Rescued

1 For details, see J.D. Webb, *How to Change the Image of Your Church* (London: SPCK, 1993; and Nashville, TN: Abingdon, 1993).

FURTHER READING

This book has stressed the importance of a direct engagement with Scripture, supported by theologically informed and imaginative reflection. This Further Reading section cites some additional works that you might find helpful.

Engaging with Scripture

The easiest way to get to grips with Scripture is to read a one-volume commentary. The following are all useful:

D.A. Carson, R.T. France, J.A. Motyer, and G.J. Wenham (eds), *New Bible Commentary* (Leicester, UK: IVP, 1994; and Downers Grove, Ill.: IVP, 1994). This is an excellent and very scholarly guide to the entire Bible, with each book being dealt with by an expert in the field.

Alister E. McGrath, *NIV Bible Commentary* (London: Hodder & Stoughton, 1995). This is based on the NIV text, and directed especially at those who are new to the Christian faith or to serious Bible study.

William Neil, *One Volume Bible Commentary* (London: Hodder & Stoughton, 1995). Originally published in 1962, this commentary is a useful and scholarly guide to its subject.

Obviously, all one-volume commentaries on the Bible suffer from a number of limitations. The most important of these is that the discussion of the meaning and relevance of any given biblical passage is severely limited by the restricted space. For this reason, you will find it useful to build up a library of commentaries on Scripture, such as those mentioned below. However, you will also find other books useful in helping you gain more from reading Scripture. The following work is strongly recommended to all interested in getting the most out of their reading of the Bible:

Gordon D. Fee and Douglas Stuart, *How to Read the Bible for all its Worth*, 2nd edn (Grand Rapids: Zondervan, 1993).

Several sets of commentaries are of interest. The *Tyndale Old Testament Commentaries* and the *Tyndale New Testament Commentaries* (Downers Grove, Ill: IVP; and Leicester, UK: IVP) are excellent 'starter' commentaries, and well worth purchasing. They include contributions by leading biblical scholars, pitched at a level suitable for the serious reader who is not (yet!) a biblical scholar.

The Bible Speaks Today series (Downers Grove, Ill: IVP; and Leicester, UK: IVP) is less concerned with issues of scholarship, and focuses on the relevance of the text to the situation of today. This series is an excellent addition to the bookshelf of any serious student of the Bible, and is especially helpful in the preparation of addresses and sermons.

Other books relate more specifically to the issue of spirituality.

The groundwork of spirituality

Peter Adam, *Roots of Contemporary Evangelical Spirituality* (Nottingham: Grove Books, 1988).

T.R. Albin, 'Spirituality', in S. Ferguson and D.F. Wright (eds), *New Dictionary of Theology* (Leicester: IVP, 1988), pp. 656–8.

Robert M. Banks, *All the Business of Life: Bringing Theology Down to Earth* (Sutherland, NSW: Albatross, 1987).

John Cockerton, *Essentials of Evangelical Spirituality* (Nottingham: Grove Books, 1994).

Cheryl Forbes, *Imagination: Embracing a Theology of Wonder* (Portland: Multnomah Press, 1989).

David Gillett, *Trust and Obey: Explorations in Evangelical Spirituality* (London: DLT, 1993).

Christopher Hingley, 'Evangelicals and Spirituality', *Themelios* (1990), pp. 86–91.

James M. Houston, 'Spirituality', in W.A. Elwell (ed.), *Evangelical Dictionary of Theology* (Grand Rapids: Baker, 1984), p. 1046.

James M. Houston, *The Transforming Friendship: A Guide to Prayer* (Batavia, Ill.: Lion, 1989).

James M. Houston, 'Reflections on Mysticism: How Valid is Evangelical Anti-mysticism?', in M. Bockmuehl and H. Burkhardt (eds), *Gott Lieben und seine Gebote halten* (Basle: Brunner Verlag, 1991), pp. 163–81.

James M. Houston, 'Spiritual Theology: The Kingdom of God in Daily Life', *Crux* 27/2 (June 1991), pp. 2–8.

James M. Houston, *The Heart's Desire: A Guide to Personal Fulfilment* (Batavia, Ill.: Lion, 1992).

Gordon James, *Evangelical Spirituality* (London: SPCK, 1991).

Alister E. McGrath, *Roots that Refresh: A Celebration of Reformation Spirituality* (London: Hodder & Stoughton, 1992); published in the United States as *Spirituality in an Age of Change: Rediscovering the Spirit of the Reformers* (Grand Rapids: Zondervan, 1994).

James I. Packer, *Knowing God* (London: Hodder & Stoughton, 1978; and Downers Grove, Ill.: IVP, 1978).

James I. Packer, 'An Introduction to Systematic Spirituality', *Crux* 26/1 (March 1990), pp. 2–8.

James I. Packer, *A Quest for Godliness: The Puritan Vision of the Christian Life* (Wheaton, Ill.: Crossway, 1990); published in the United Kingdom as *Among God's Giants: Aspects of Puritan Christianity* (Eastbourne: Kingsway, 1991).

David Parker, 'Evangelical Spirituality Reviewed', *Evangelical Quarterly* 63 (1991), pp. 123–48.

Eugene H. Peterson, *A Long Obedience in the Same Direction: Discipleship in an Instant Society* (Downers Grove, Ill.: IVP, 1980).

Eugene H. Peterson, *Reversed Thunder: The Revelation of John and the Praying Imagination* (San Francisco: Harper & Row, 1988).

Edward C. Sellner, 'C.S. Lewis as Spiritual Mentor', in L. Byrne (ed.), *Traditions of Spiritual Guidance* (Collegeville, MN: Liturgical Press, 1990), pp. 142–61.

Donald S. Whitney, *Spiritual Disciplines for the Christian Life* (Colorado Springs: NavPress, 1991).

Alister McGrath has written many popular books, such as *Explaining Your Faith, Spirituality in an Age of Change, Suffering and God, The Mystery of the Cross,* and *The Sunnier Side of Doubt.* He became a Christian while a student at Oxford University. He was a pastor in Nottingham during the early 1980s, and he is often invited to preach in various pulpits.

He is a professor of theology at Wycliffe Hall, Oxford, at Oxford University, and at Regent College (Vancouver, British Columbia). Among his many scholarly titles are *A Life of John Calvin, Luther's Theology of the Cross, Reformation Thought,* and *The Intellectual Origins of the European Reformation.*